Nurit Karlin's world
is a collection of
captionless cartoons
that delight the eye
and go straight to
the heart.
Animals, kings, musicians,
centipedes, and plants live
topsy-turvy lives in
sublime silence and
total madness.

Nurit Karlin was born in Jerusalem. After her graduation from the Bezalel School of Art she worked as a commercial artist in Israel before coming to the United States to study at the School of Visual Arts in New York, where she continues to live and work. In 1973, she began submitting her drawings, which have appeared in a variety of publications, including the *New Yorker,* the *New York Times, National Enquirer, Saturday Review,* and *Ladies' Home Journal.*

NO
COMMENT

CARTOONS by
NURIT KARLIN

BANTAM BOOKS
Toronto / New York / London / Sydney

NO COMMENT

*A Bantam Book / published by arrangement with
Charles Scribner's Sons*

*PRINTING HISTORY
Scribner's edition published September 1978*

Bantam edition / September 1981

Of the 127 drawings in this collection, 38 originally appeared in the New Yorker, copyright © 1974, 1975, 1976, 1977 by the New Yorker Magazine, Inc.; two drawings apiece are from the Saturday Review and the National Enquirer, copyright © 1977 the Saturday Review and copyright © 1976, 1977 the National Enquirer.

*All rights reserved.
Copyright © 1978 by Nurit Karlin.
Copyright under the Berne Convention.
This book may not be reproduced in whole or in part, by mimeograph or any other means, without permission.
For information address: Charles Scribner's Sons,
597 Fifth Avenue, New York, N.Y. 10017.*

ISBN 0-553-20210-3

Published simultaneously in the United States and Canada

Bantam Books are published by Bantam Books, Inc. Its trademark, consisting of the words "Bantam Books" and the portrayal of a bantam, is Registered in U.S. Patent and Trademark Office and in other countries. Marca Registrada. Bantam Books, Inc., 666 Fifth Avenue, New York, New York 10103.

PRINTED IN THE UNITED STATES OF AMERICA

0 9 8 7 6 5 4 3 2 1

To Henry Martin with gratitude

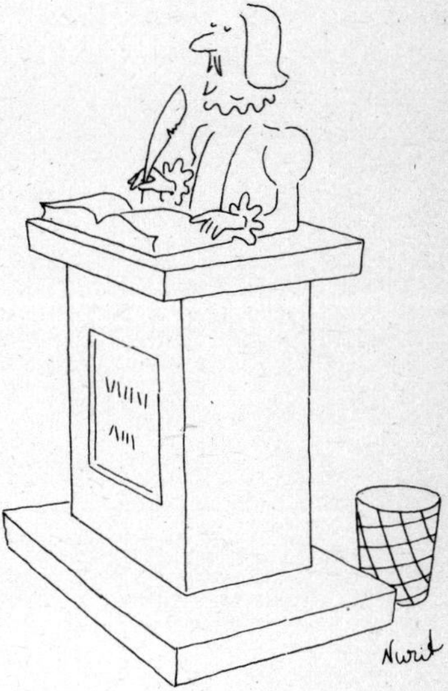
Nurit

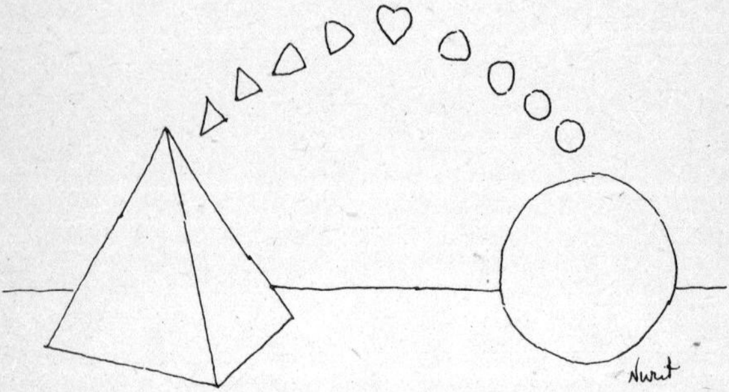
Nurit

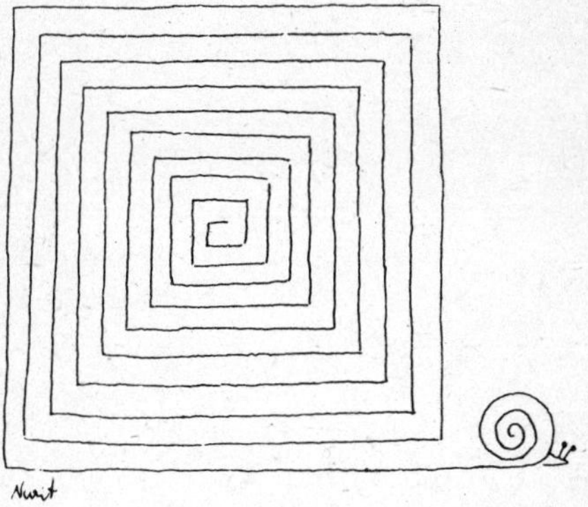
Nurit

THIS SIDE UP
THIS SIDE UP
THIS SIDE UP
THIS SIDE UP

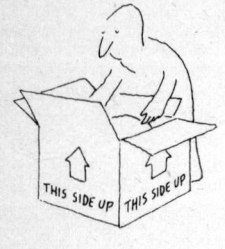

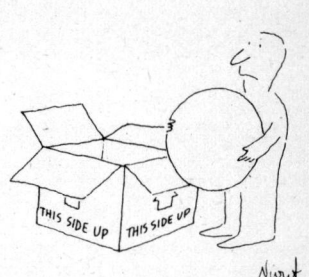

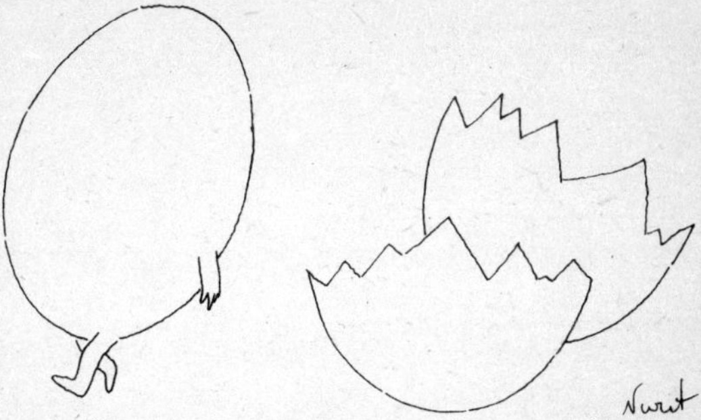
Nurit

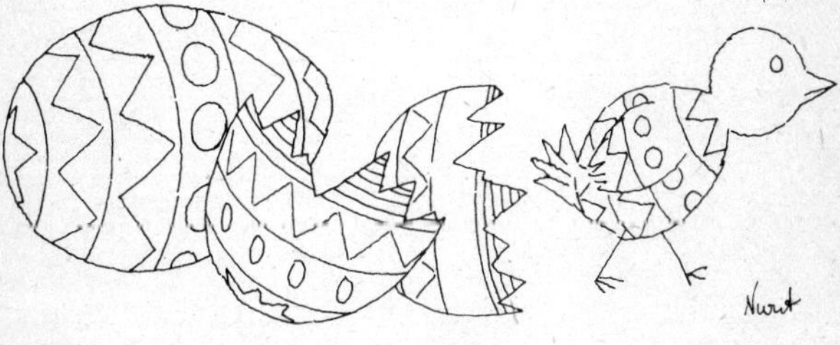
Nurit

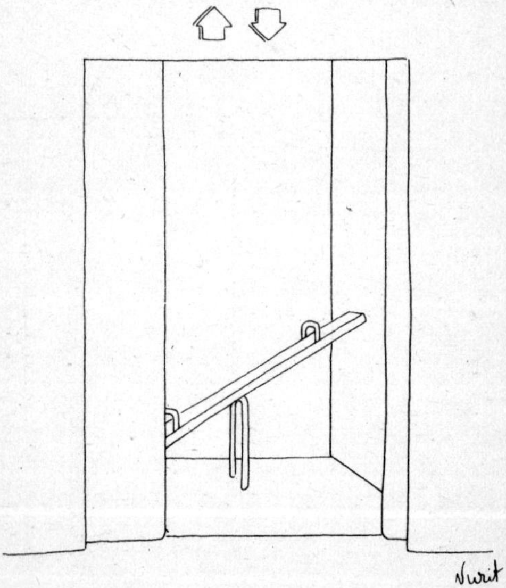
Nurit

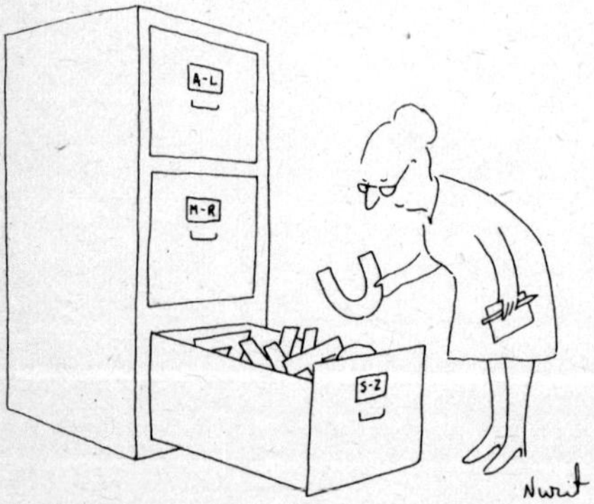
A-L
M-R
S-Z
Nurit

INFORMATION
Nurit

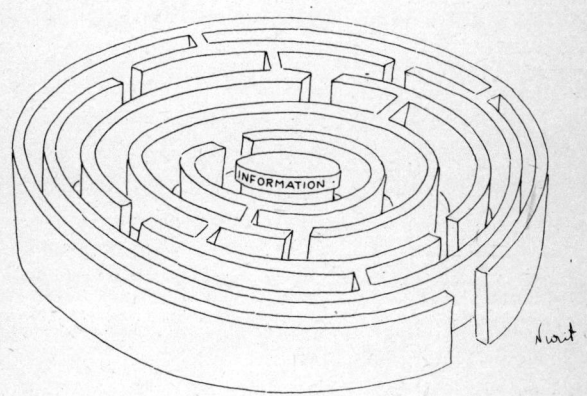

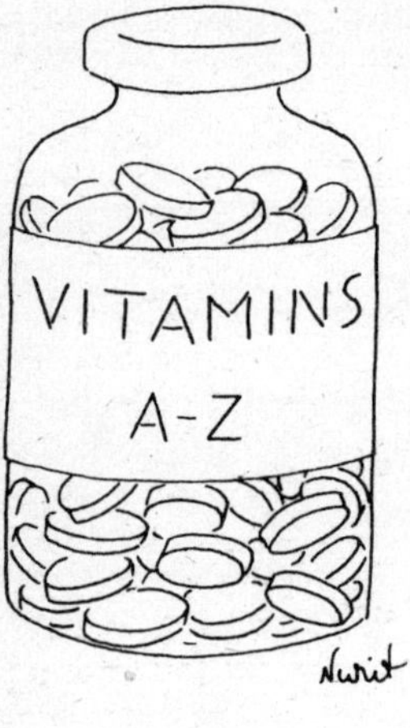
VITAMINS
A-Z
Nurit

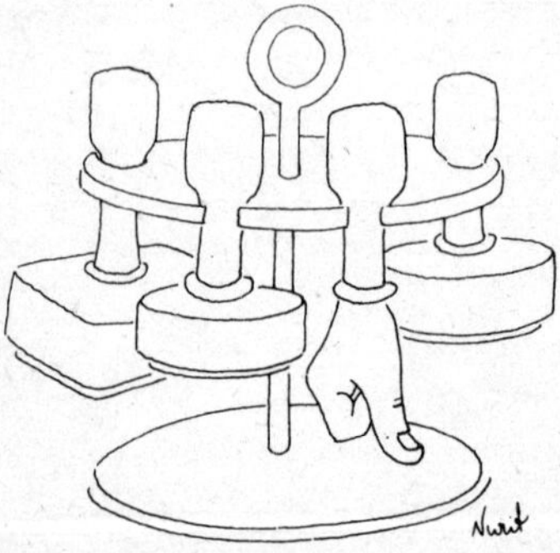
Nurit

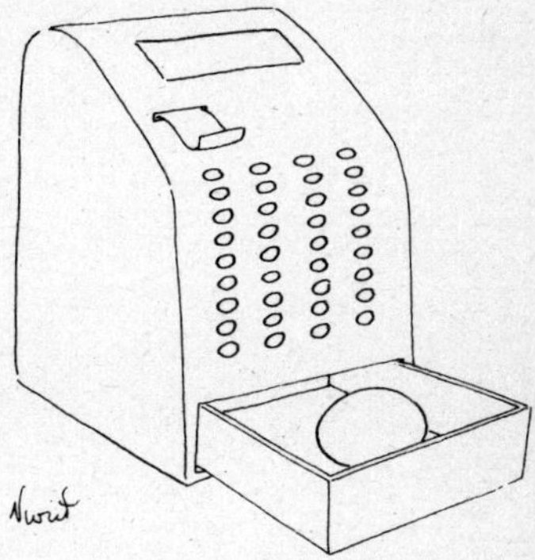
Nurit

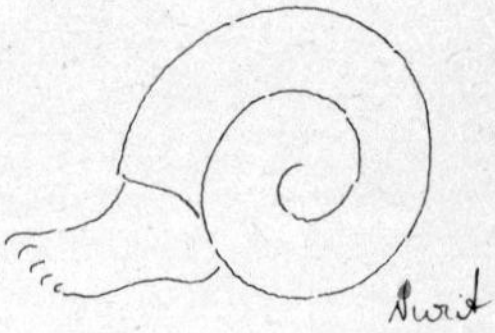
Nurit

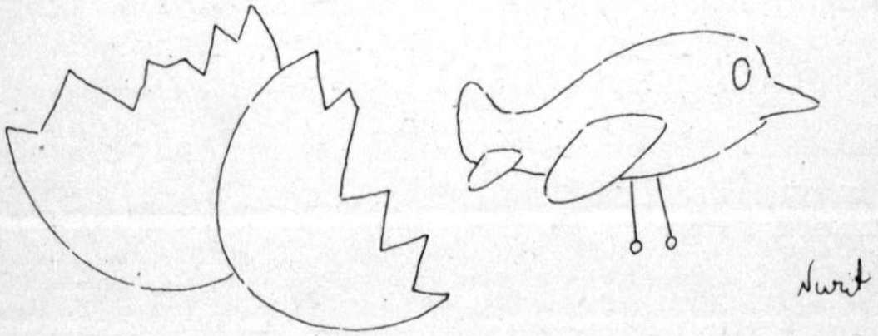
Nurit

FOR
RENT
Nurit

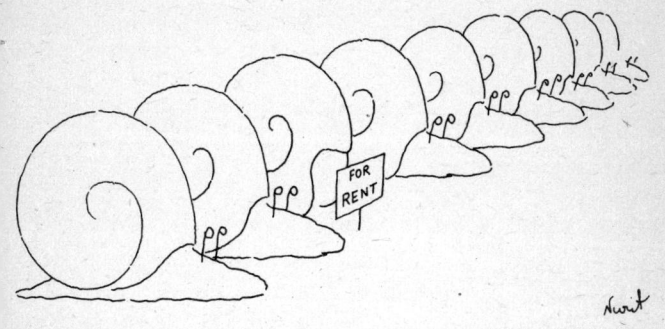

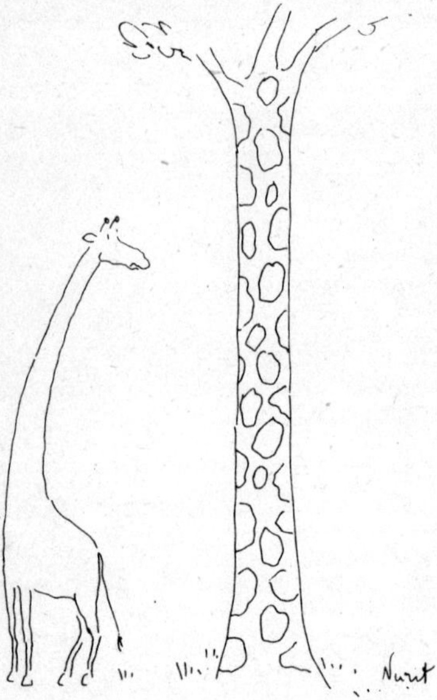
Nurit

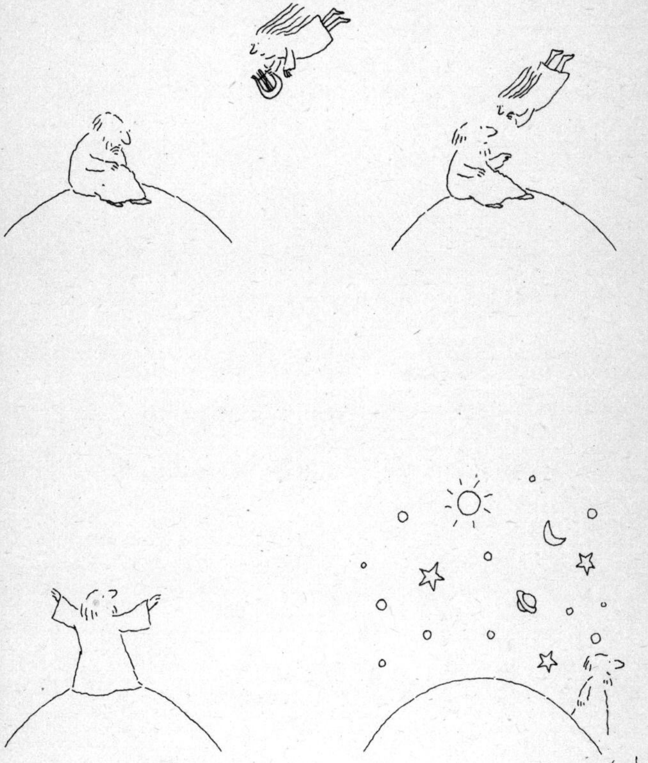
Nurit

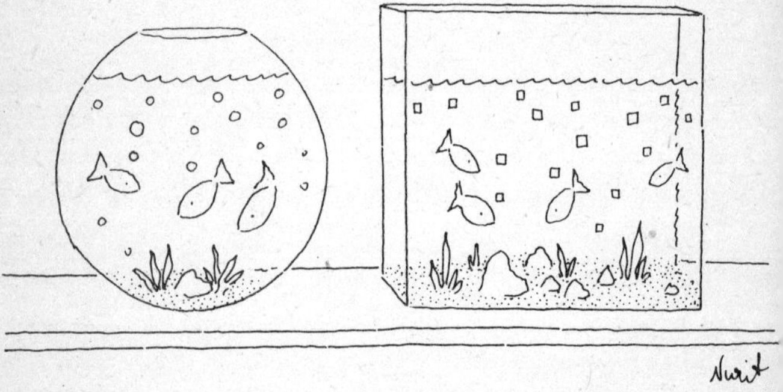
Nurit

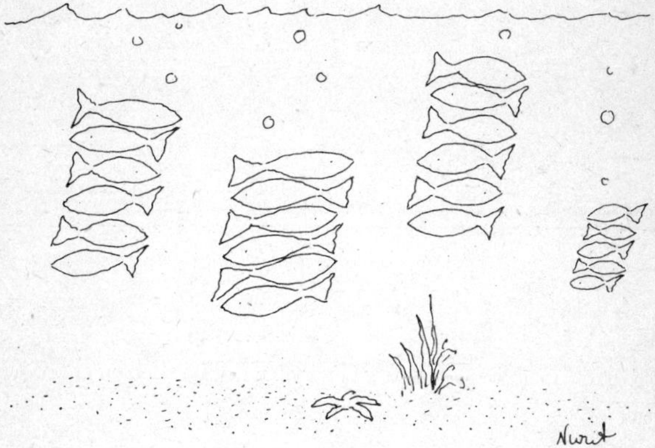
Nurit

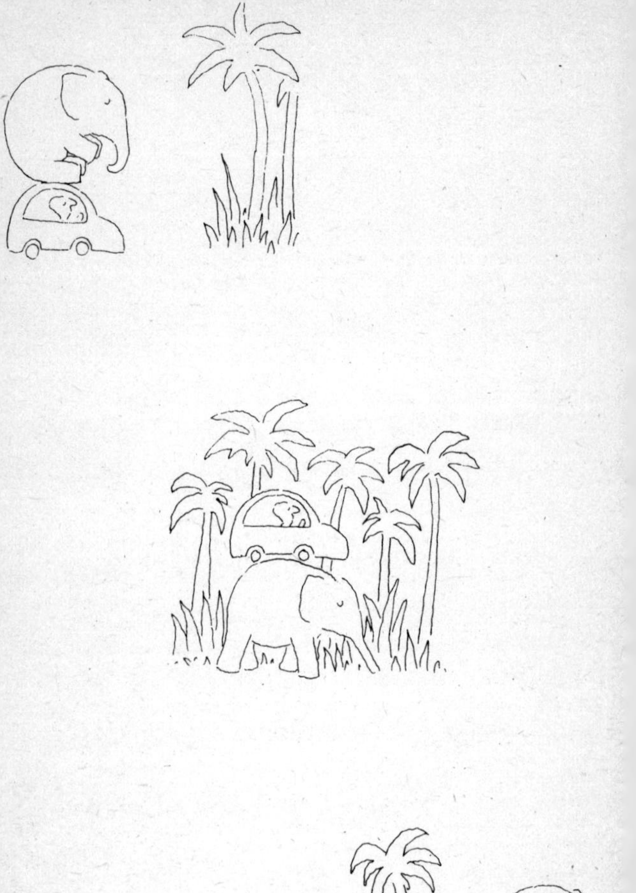

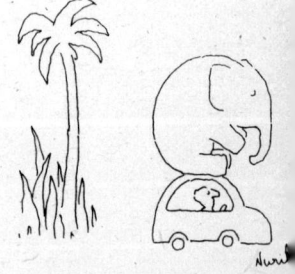

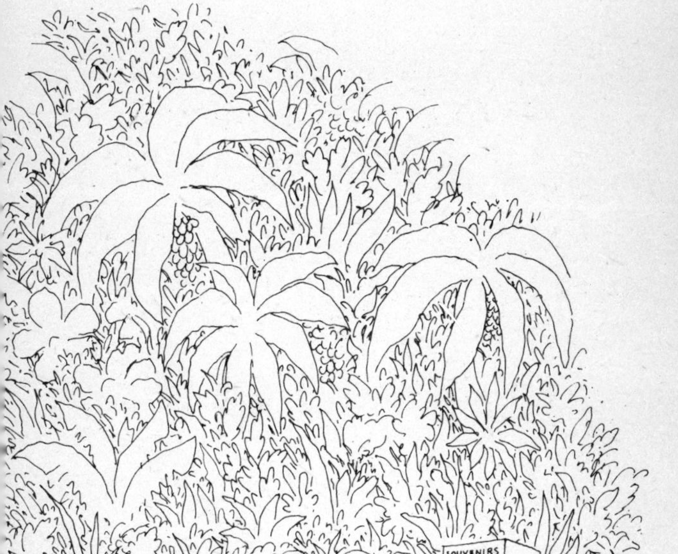
SOUVENIRS
Nurit

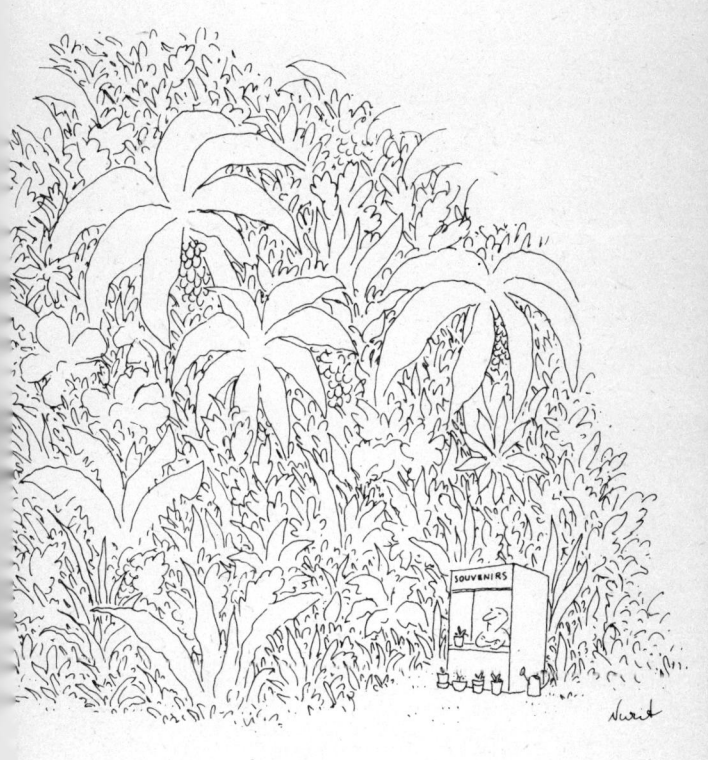

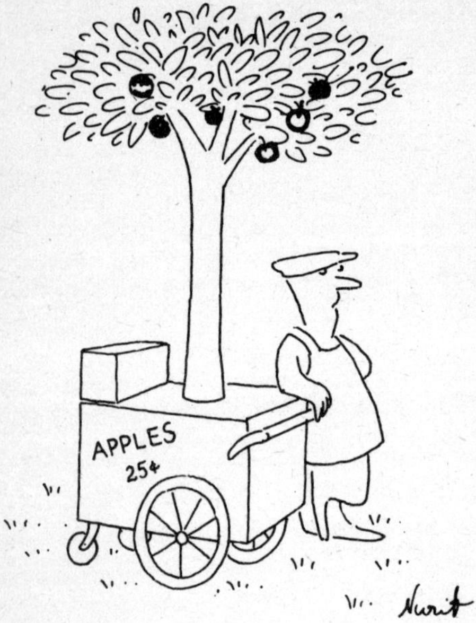
APPLES
25¢
Nurit

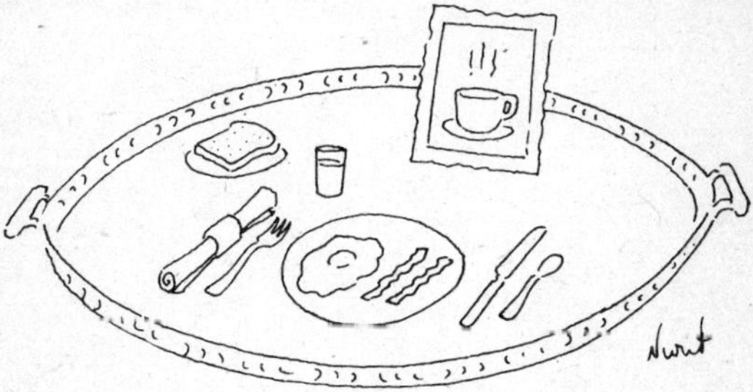
Nurit

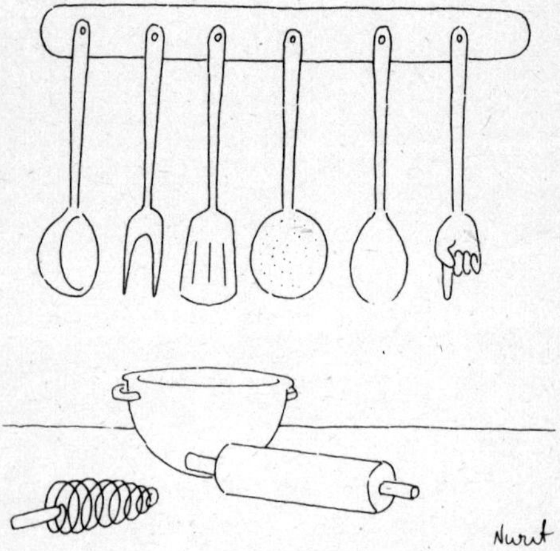
Nurit

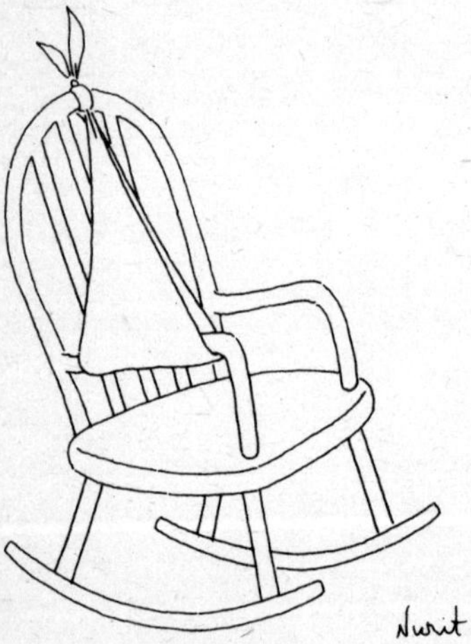
Nurit

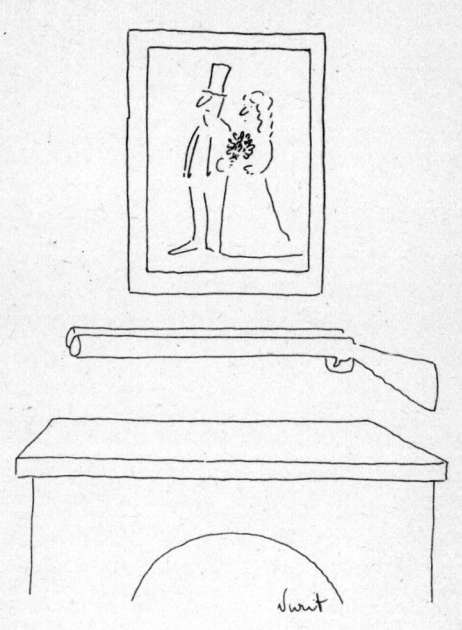

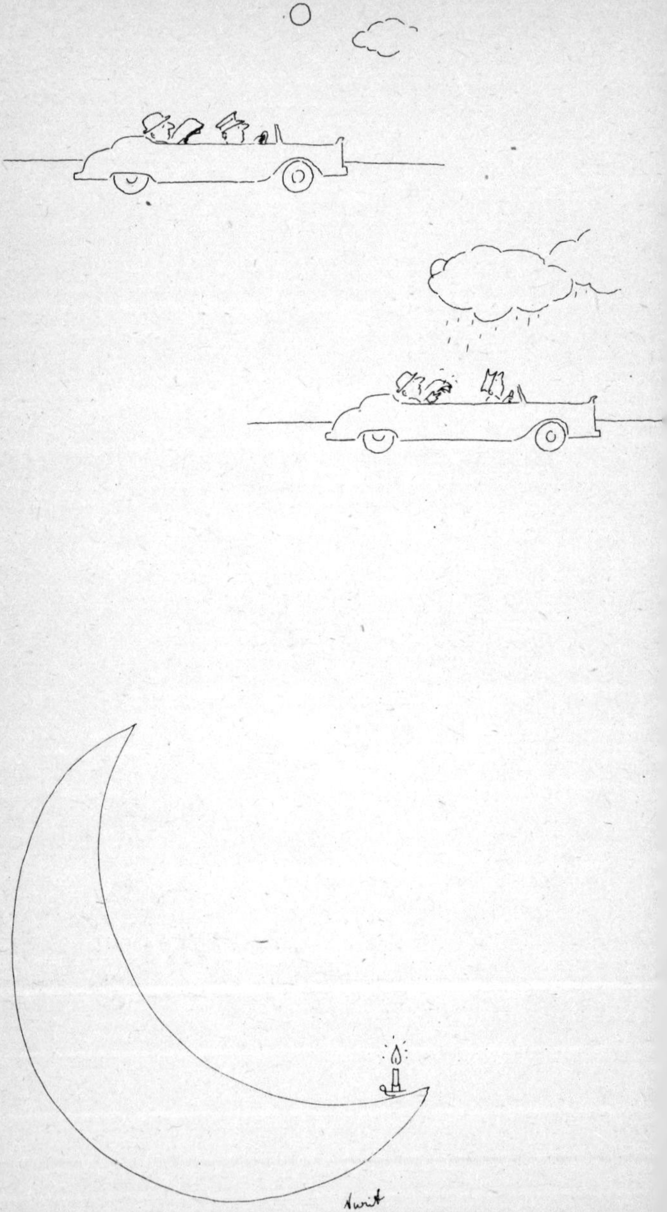
Nurit

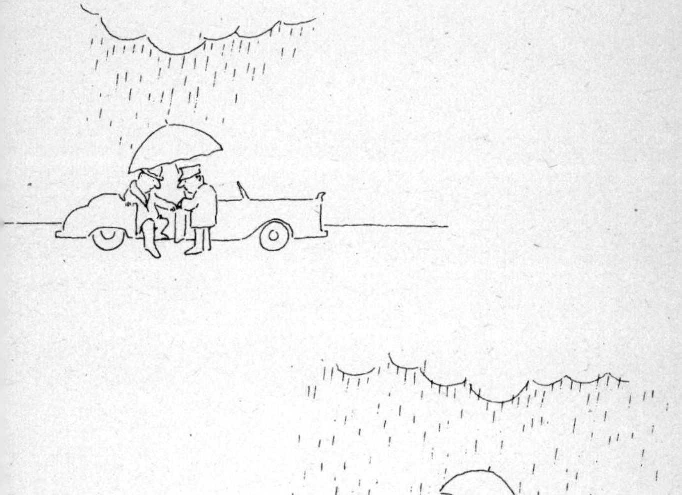
Nurit

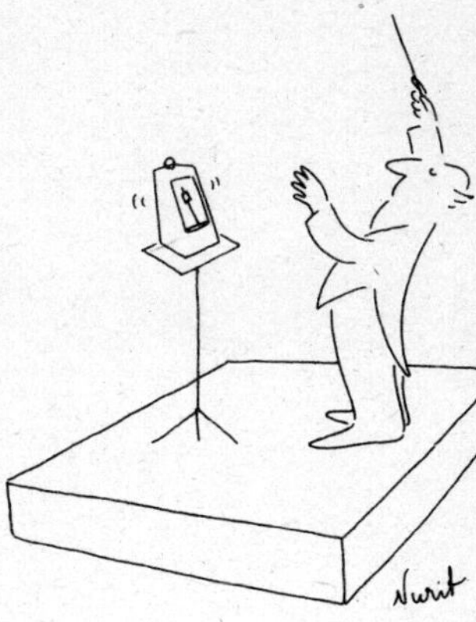
Nurit

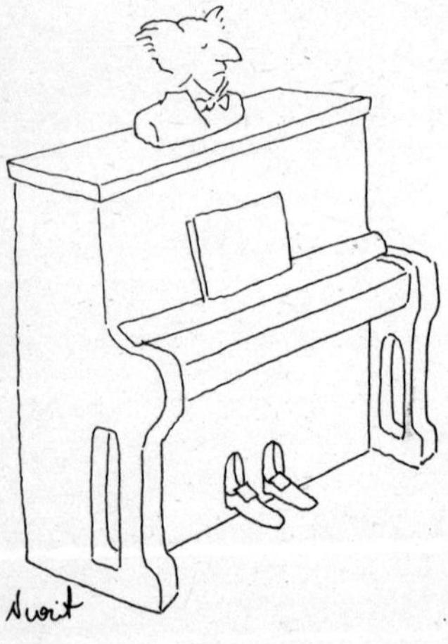
Nurit

Nurit

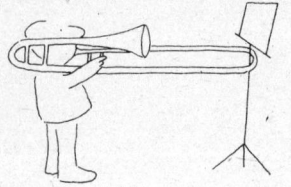

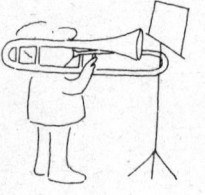

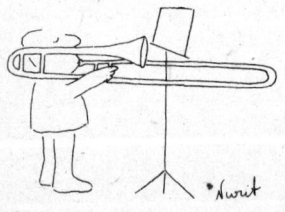

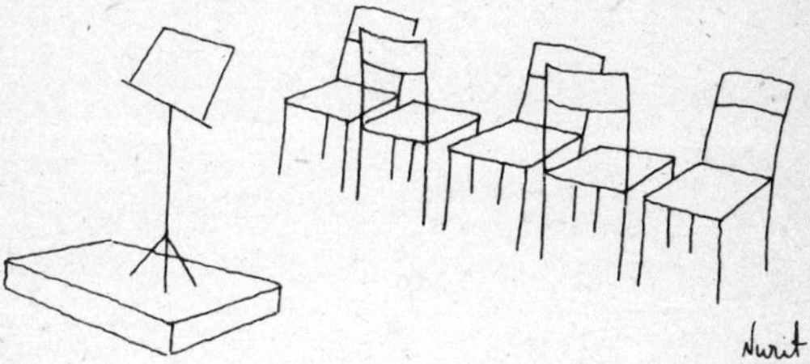
Nurit

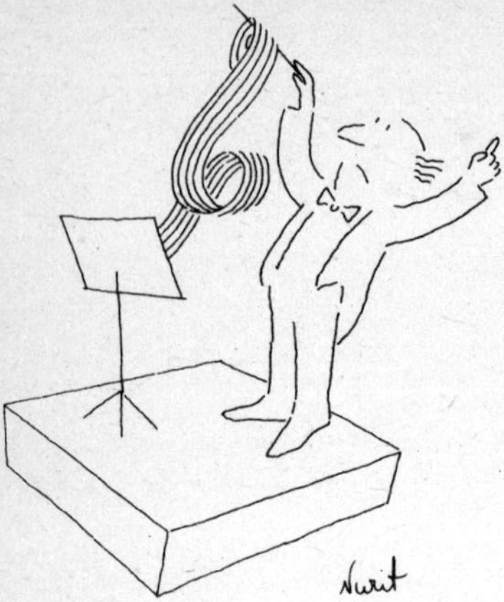
Nurit

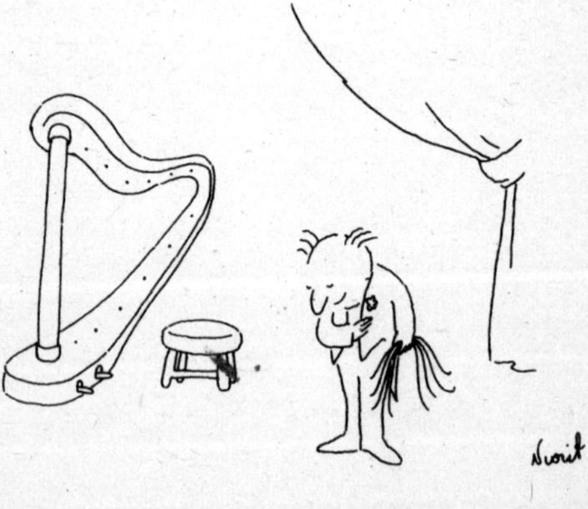
Nurit

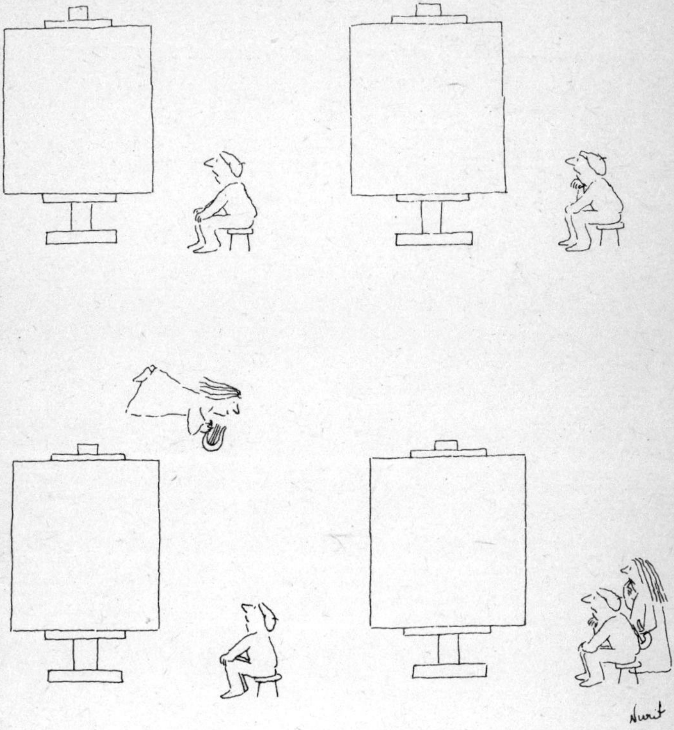
Nurit

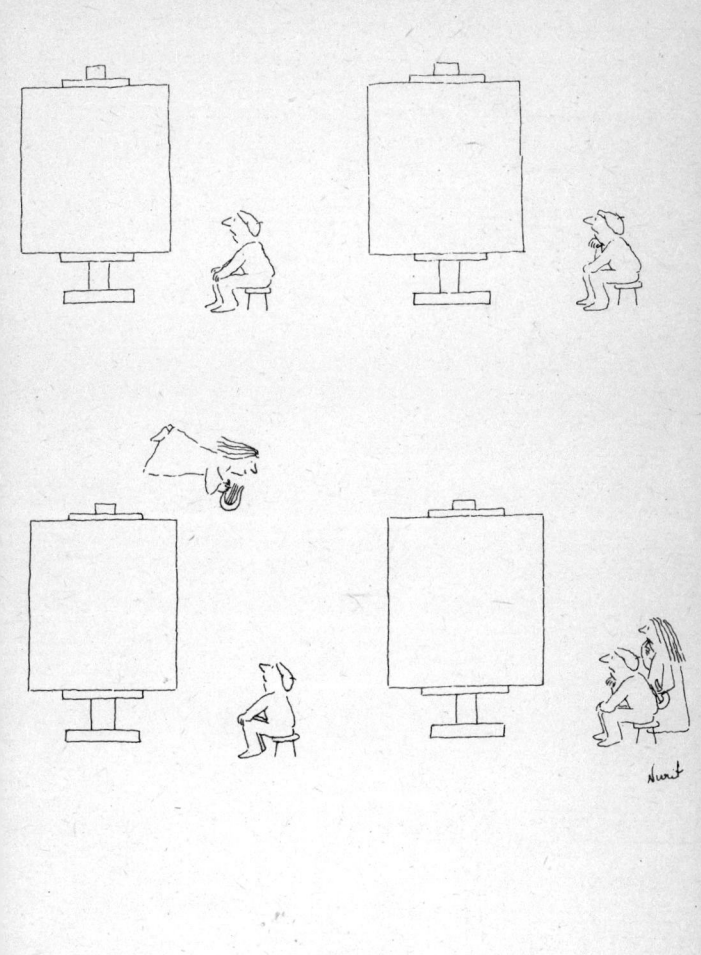

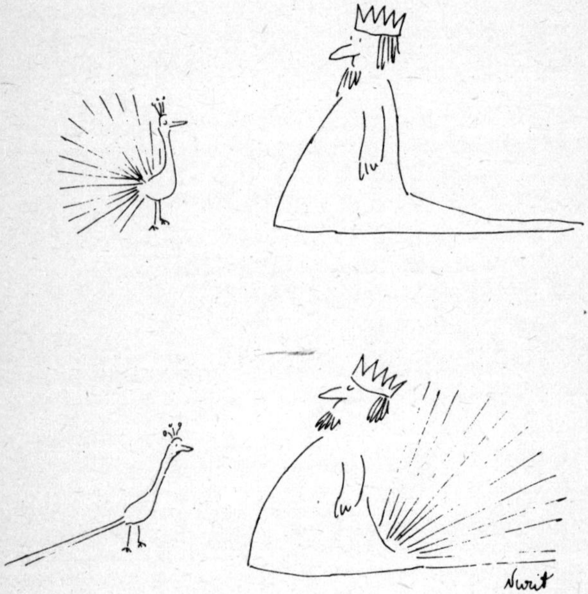
Nurit

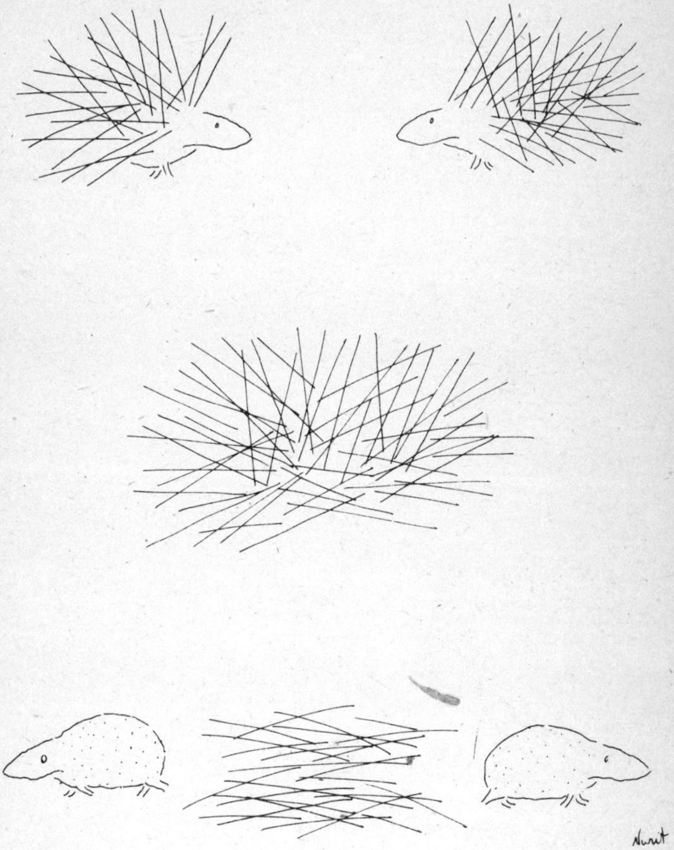
Nurit

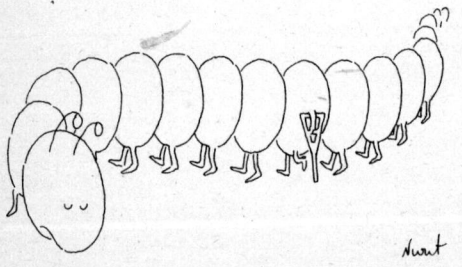

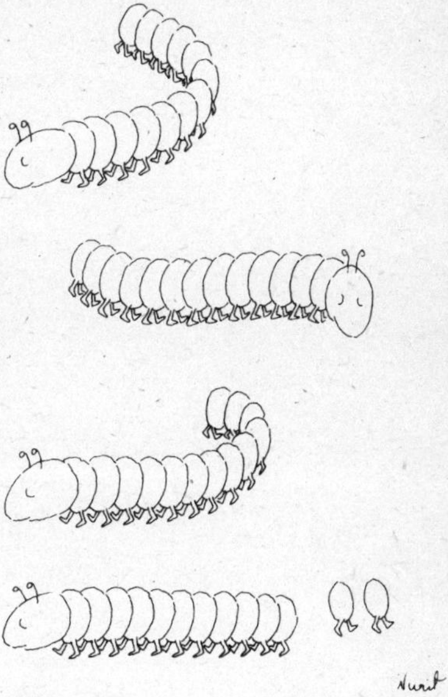
Nurit

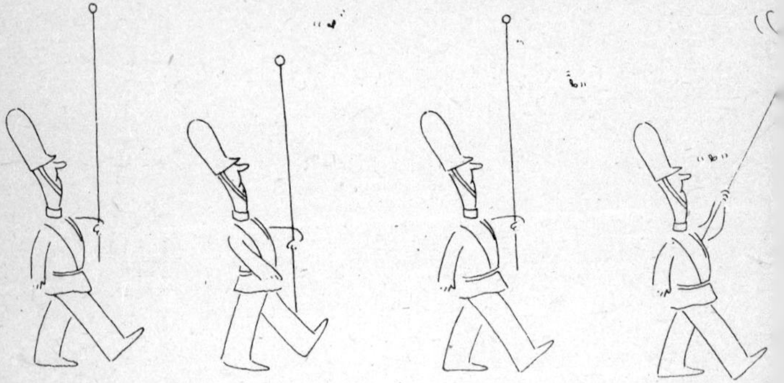

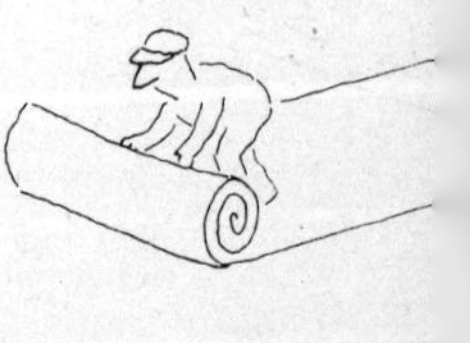

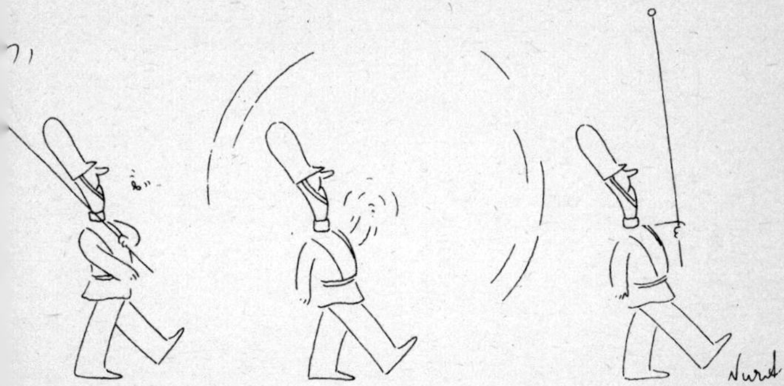
Nurit

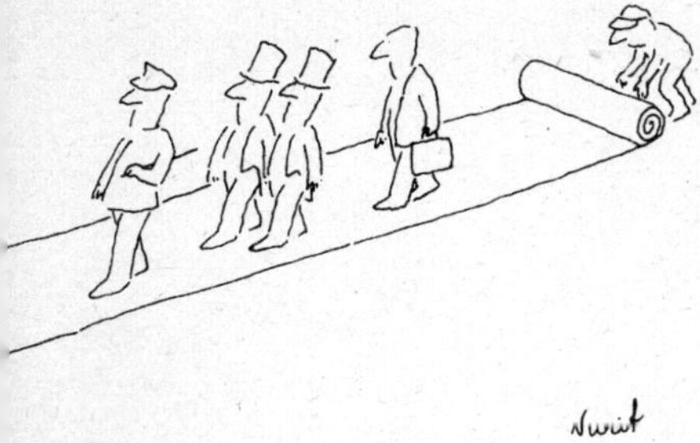
Nurit

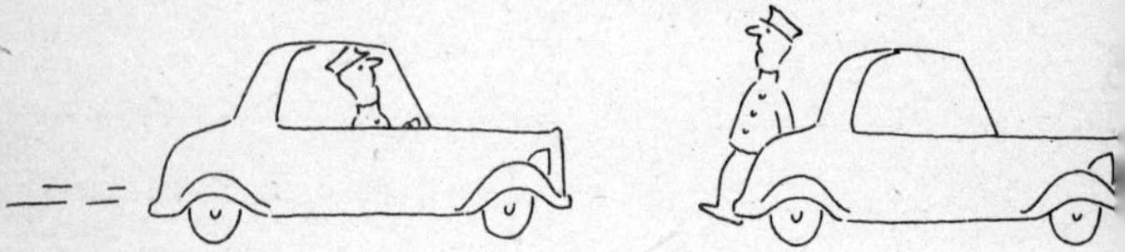

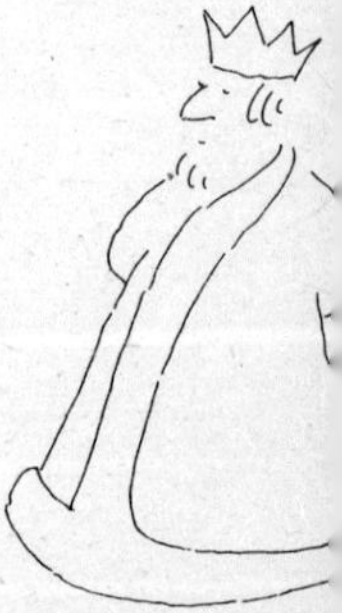

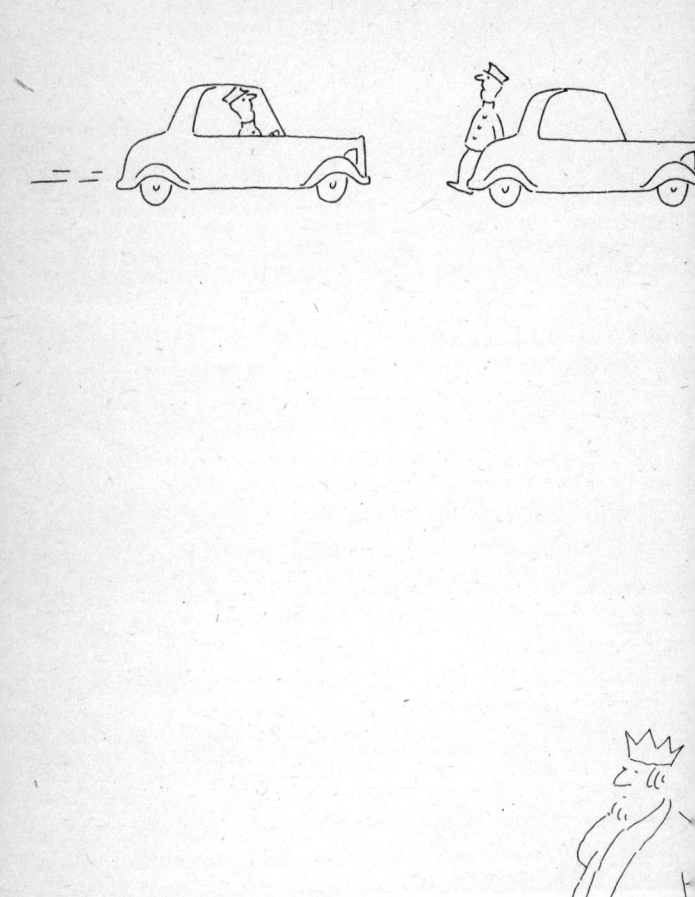

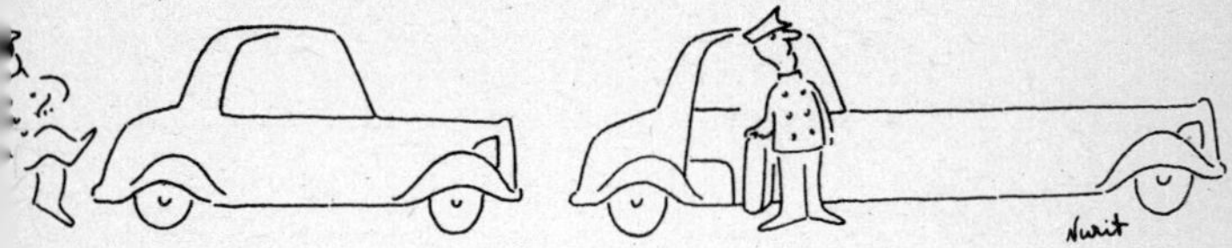
Nurit

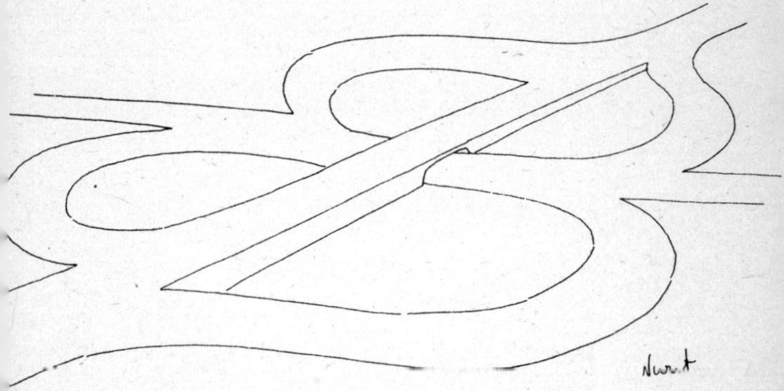
Nurit

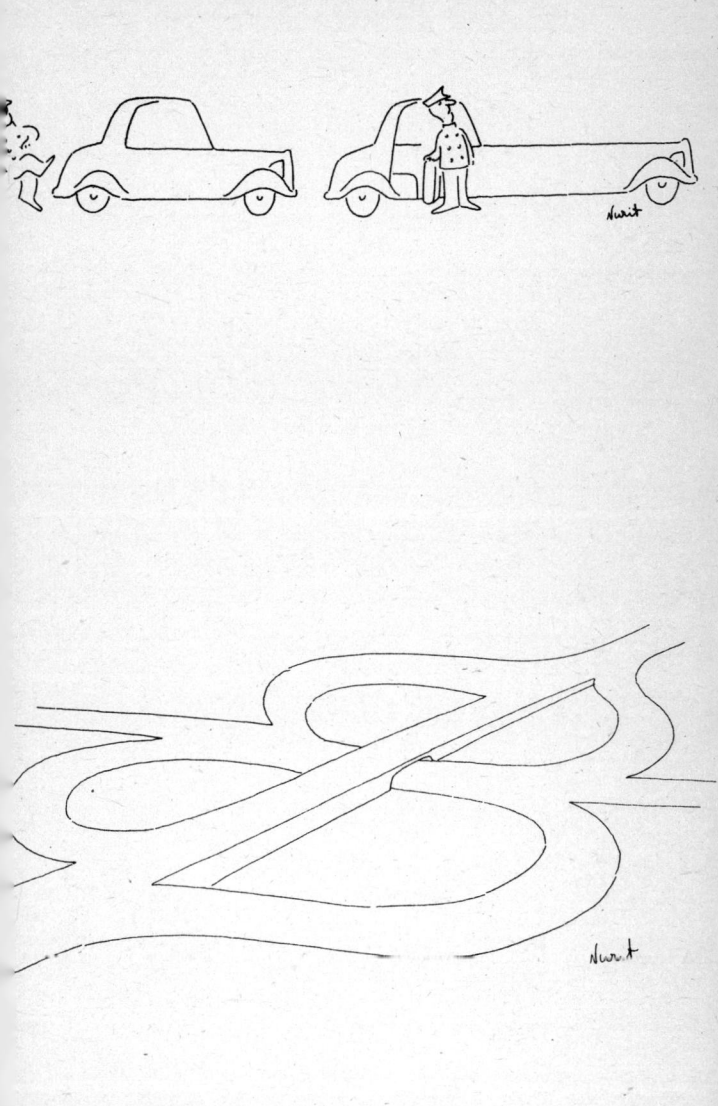

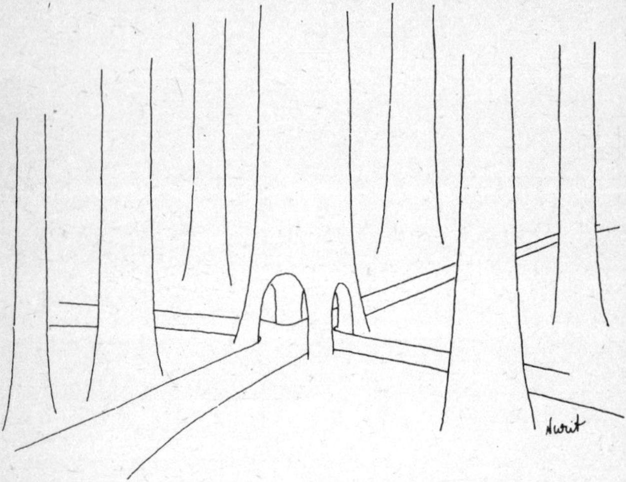
Nurit

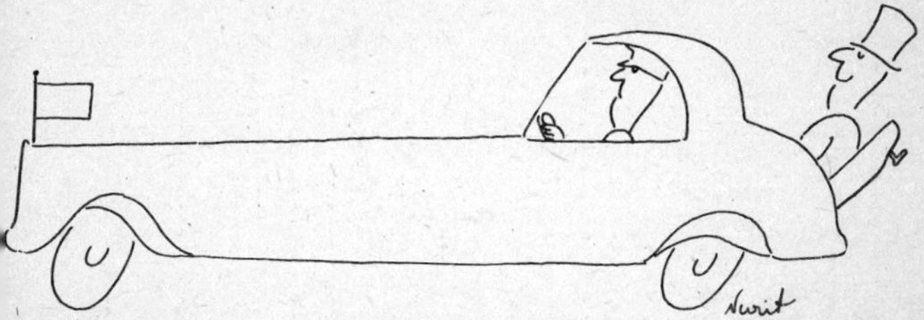
Nurit

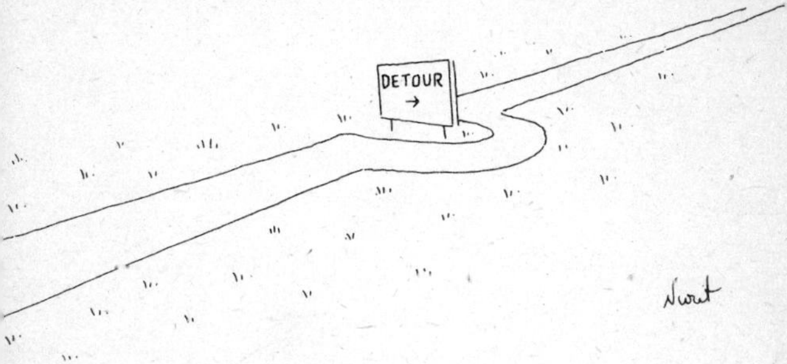
DETOUR
→
Nurit

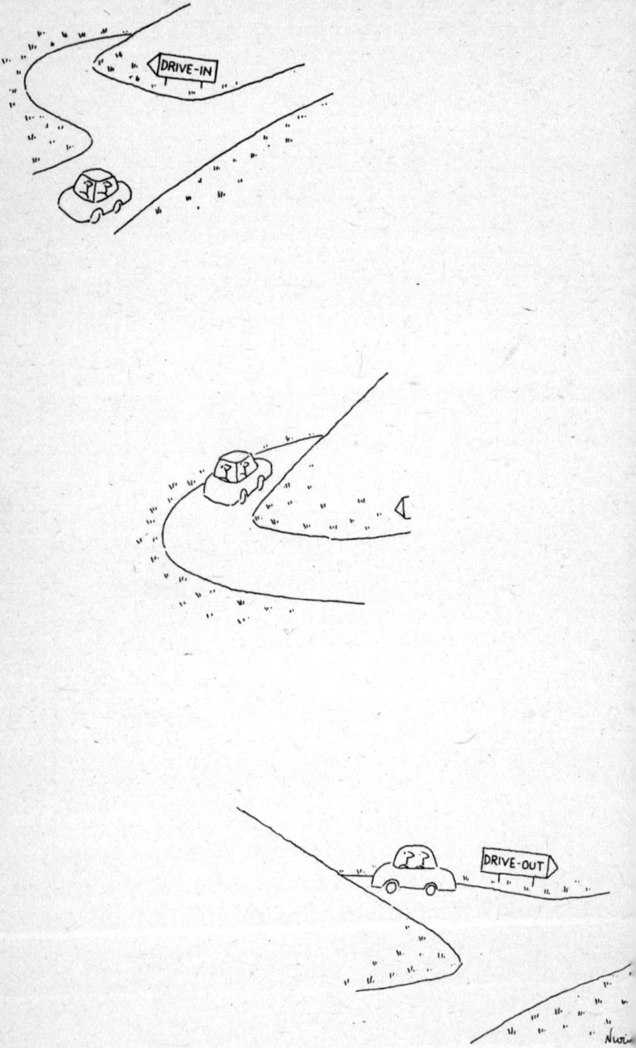
DRIVE-IN
DRIVE-OUT

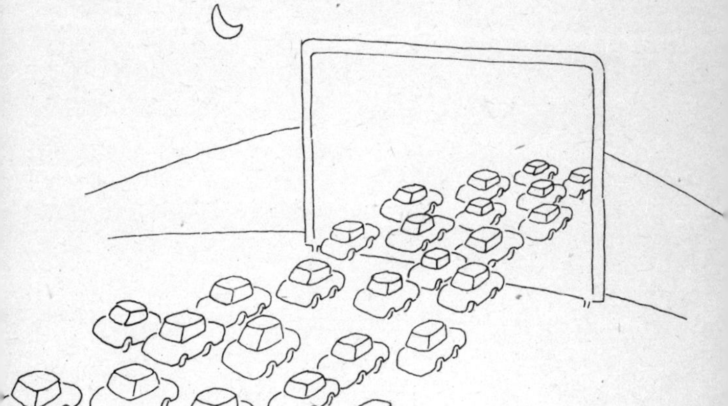
DRIVE-IN
Nurit

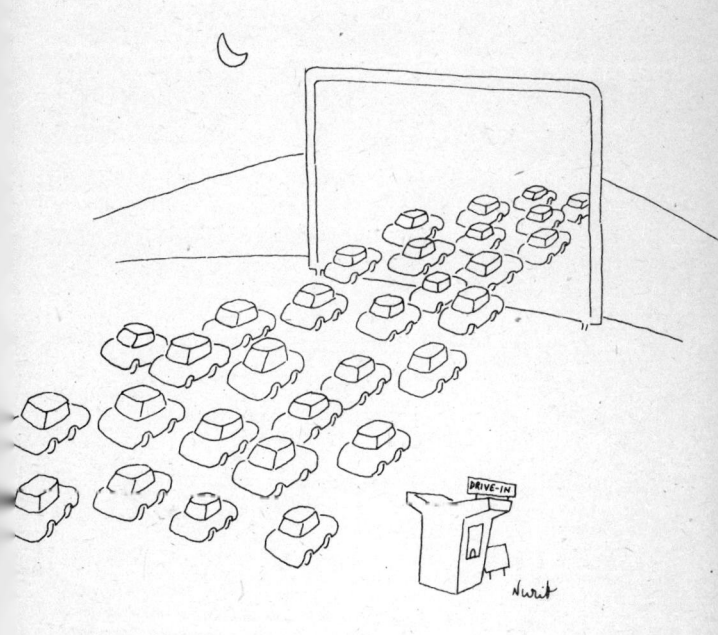

Nurit

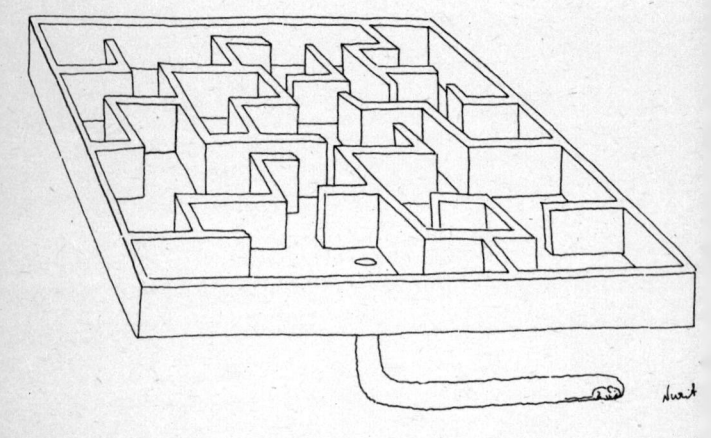

Nurit

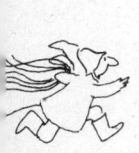

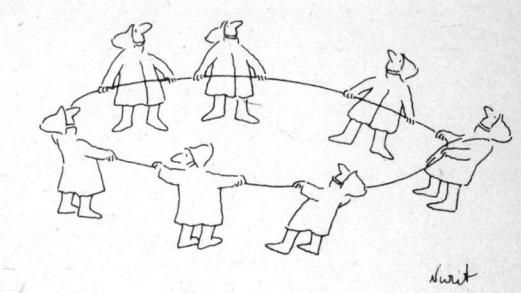

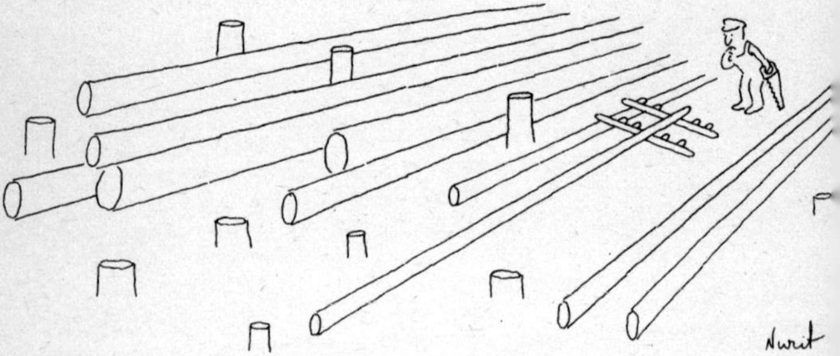
Nurit

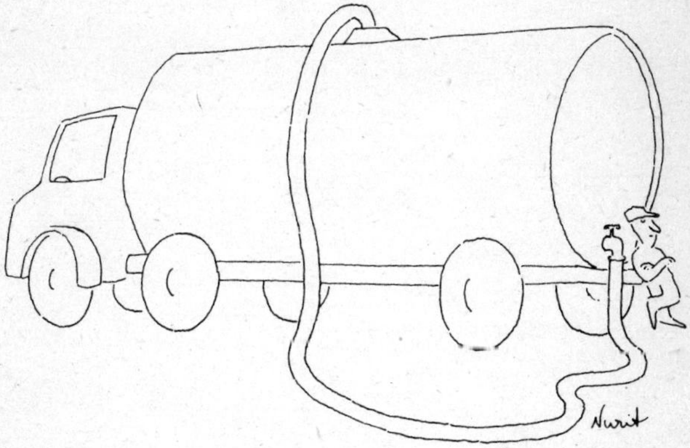
Nurit

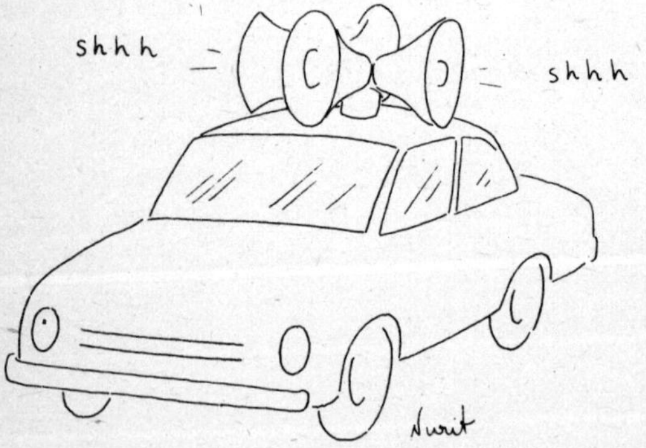
shhh
shhh
Nurit

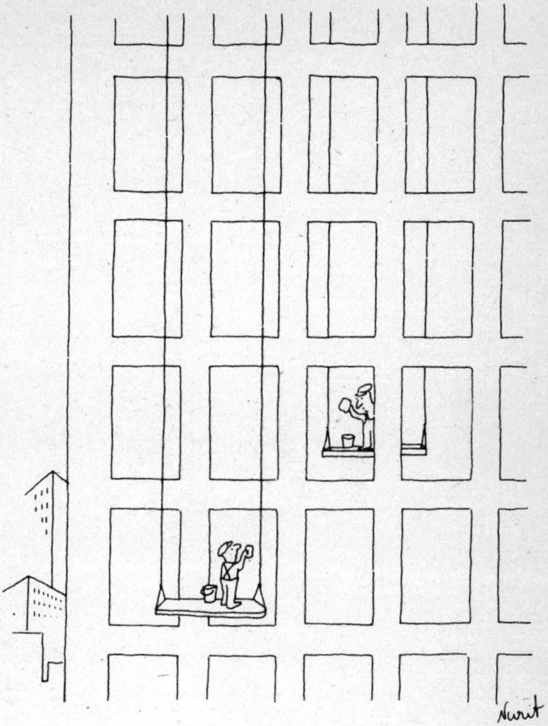
Nurit

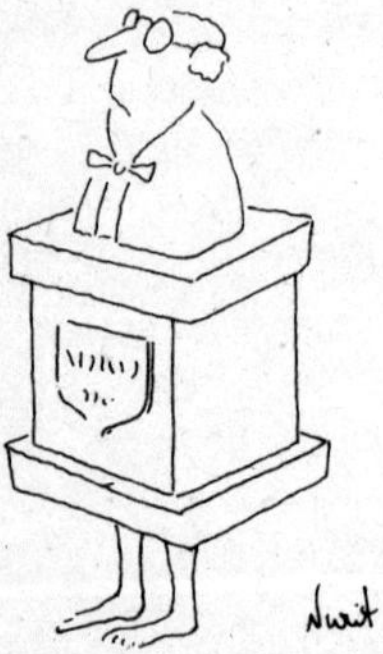
Nurit

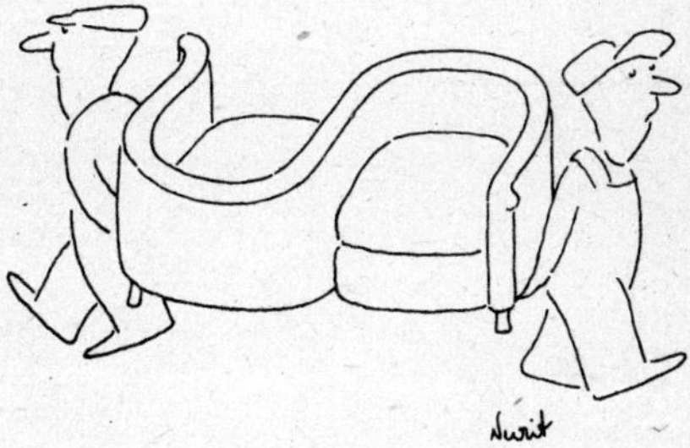
Nurit

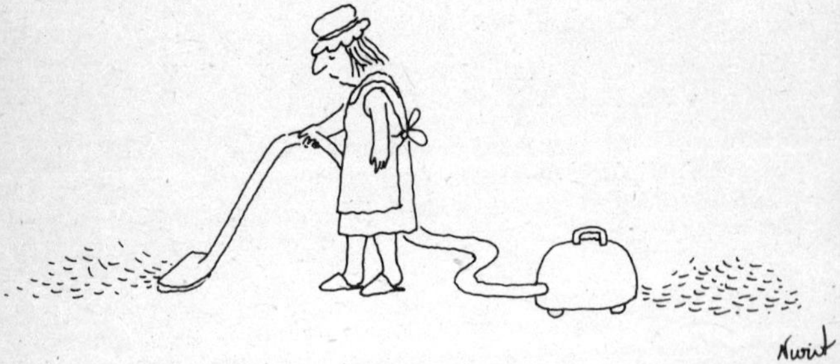
Nurit

Nurit

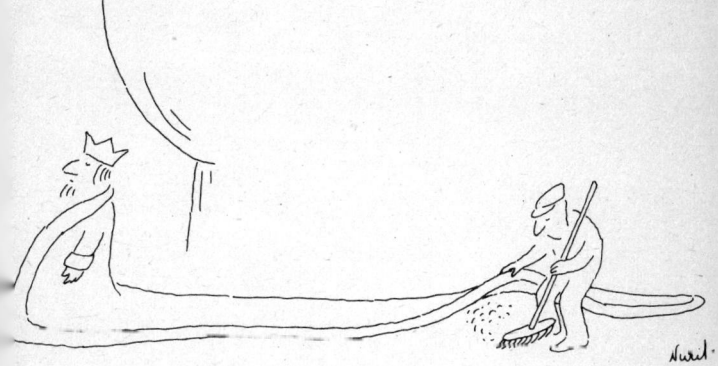

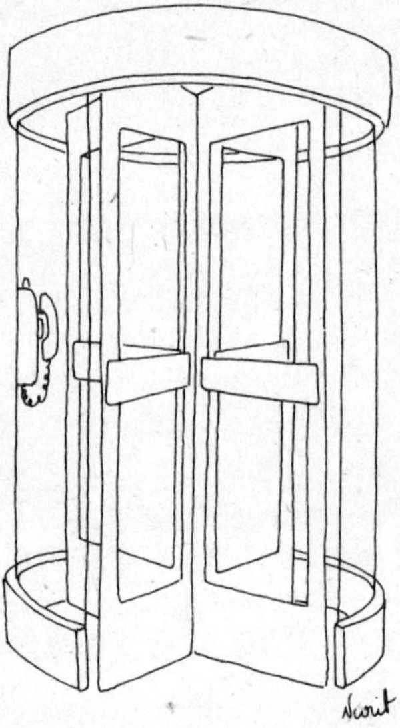
Nurit

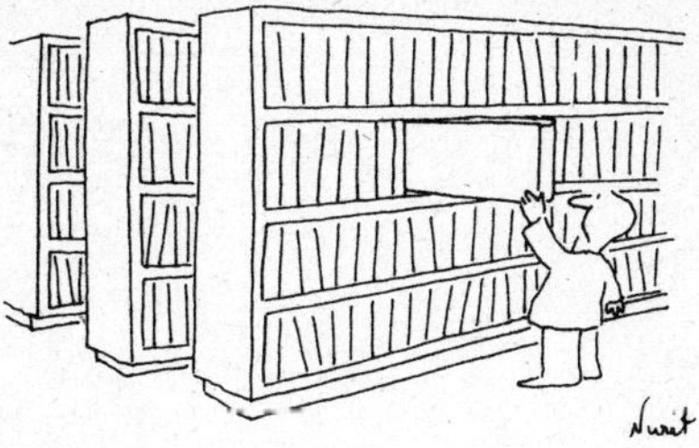
Nurit

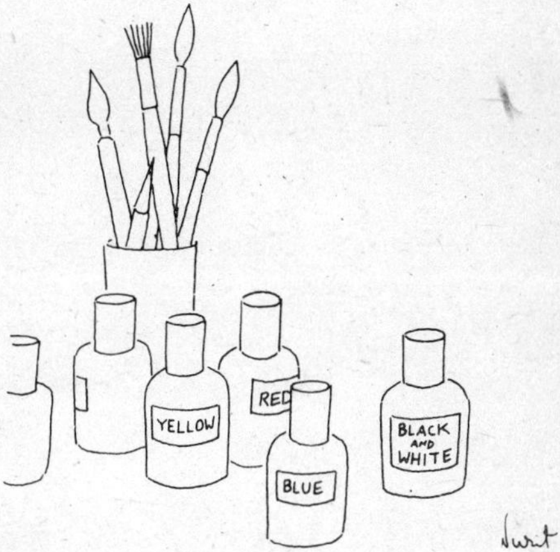
RED
YELLOW
BLUE
BLACK AND WHITE

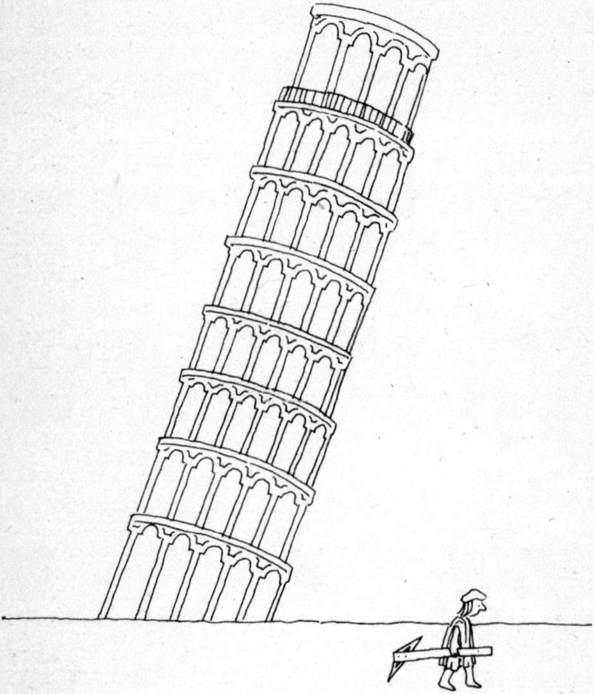
Nurit

Nurit

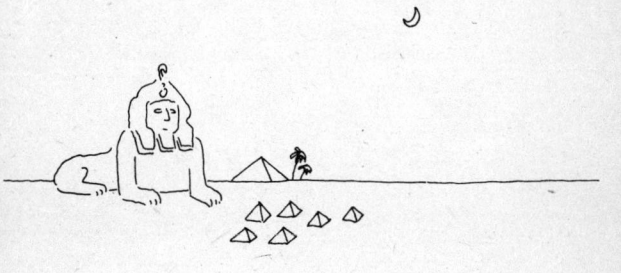

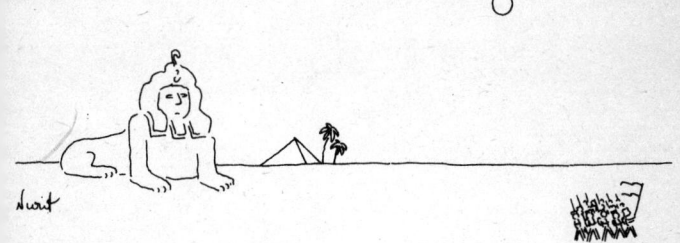

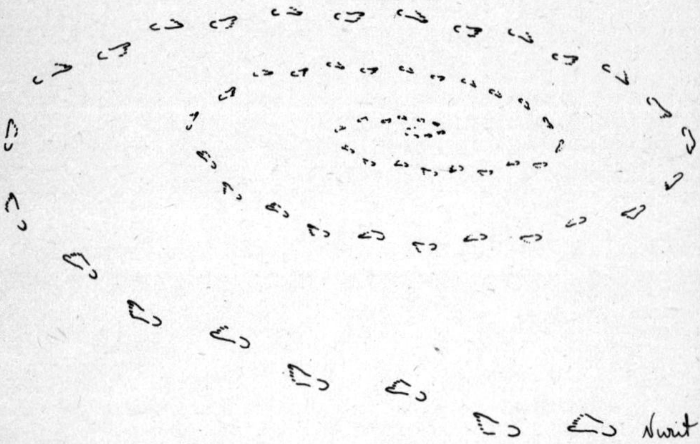
Nuvit

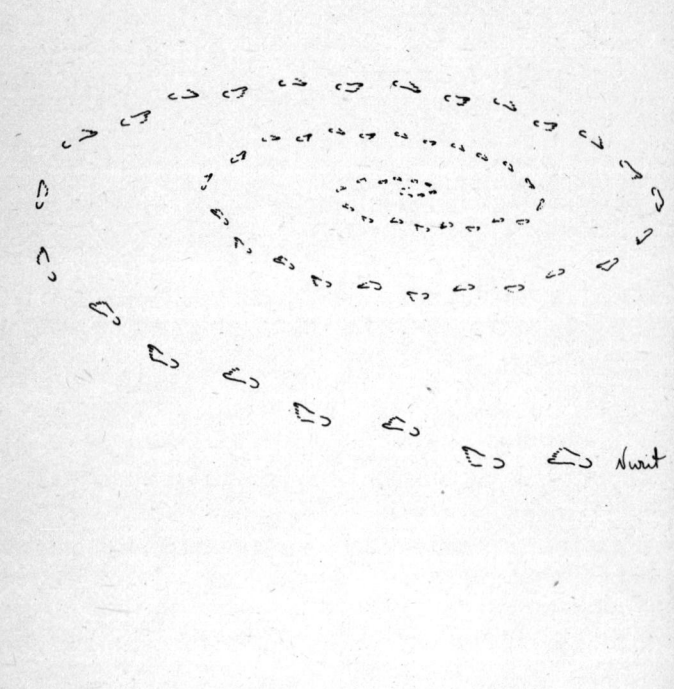

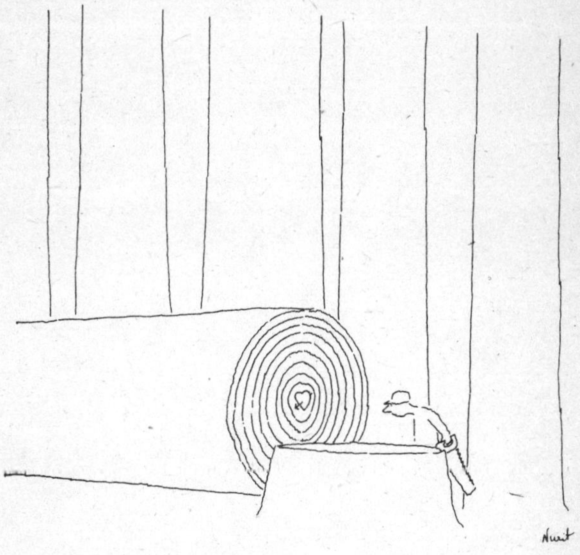
Nurit

Nurit

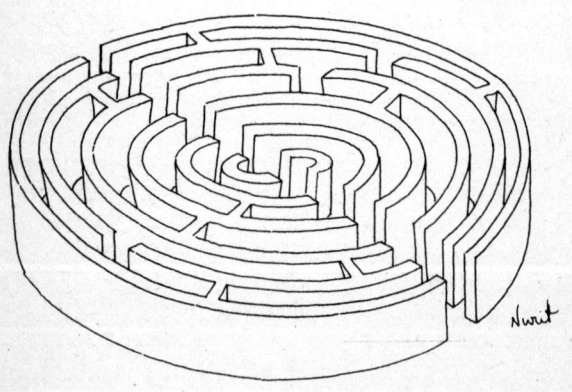

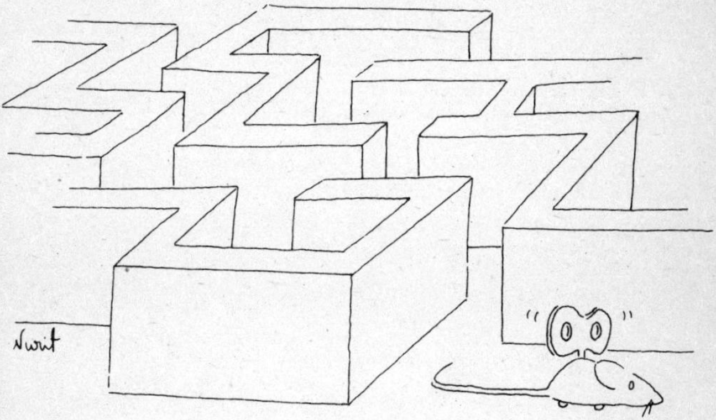
Nurit

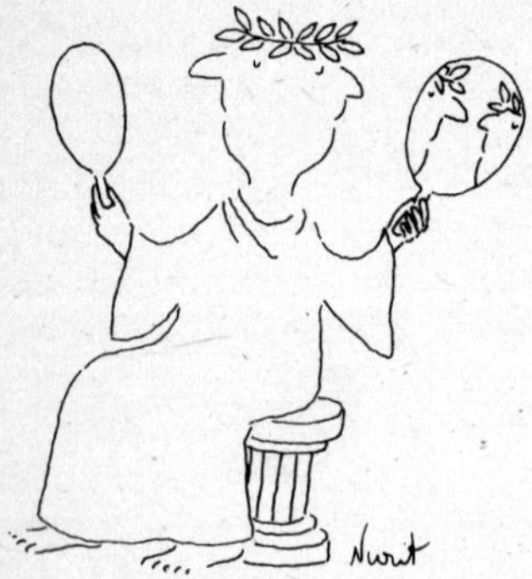
Nurit

Nurit

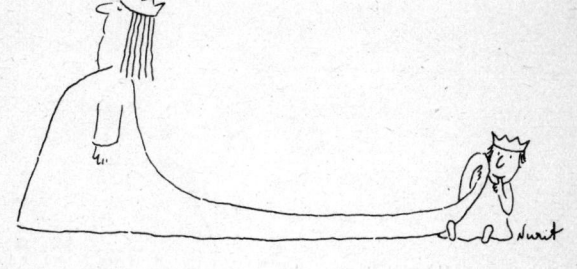

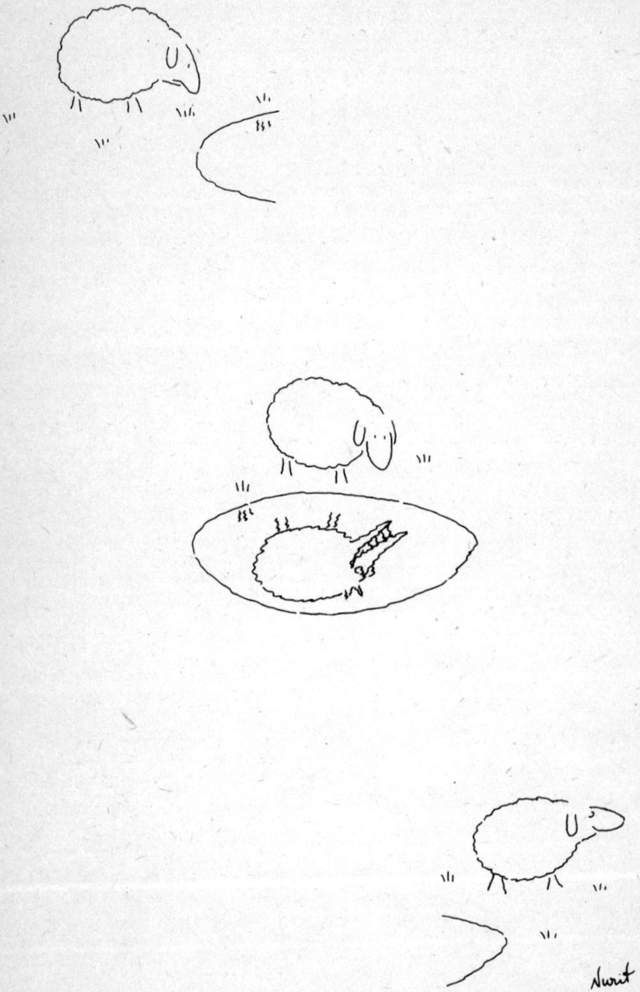
Nurit

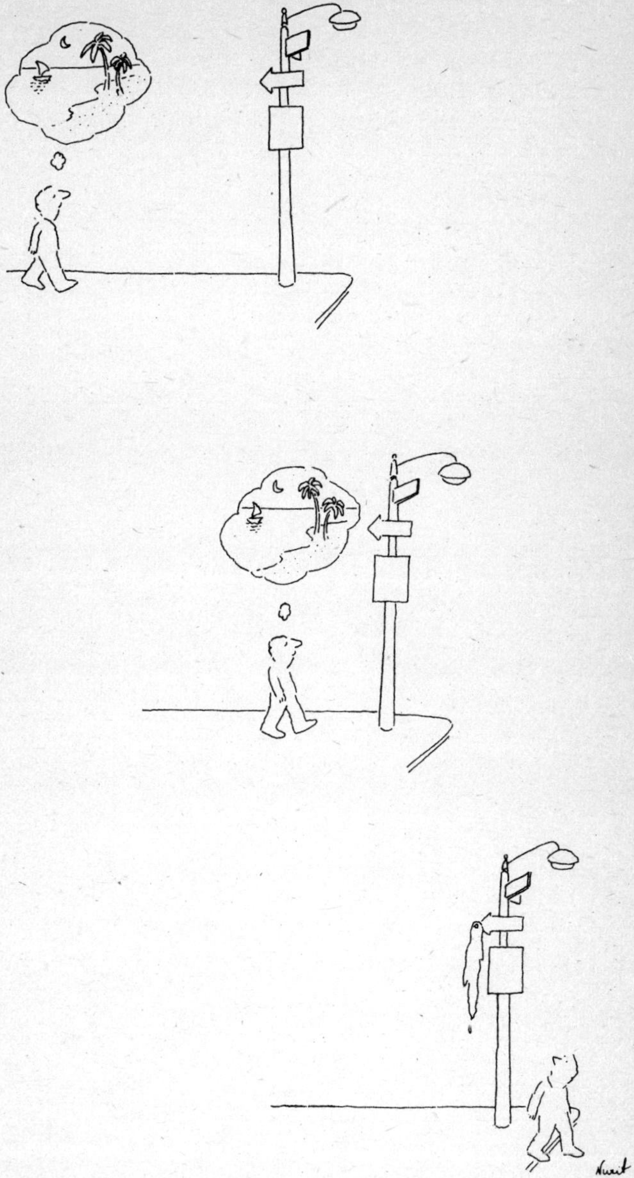
Nurit

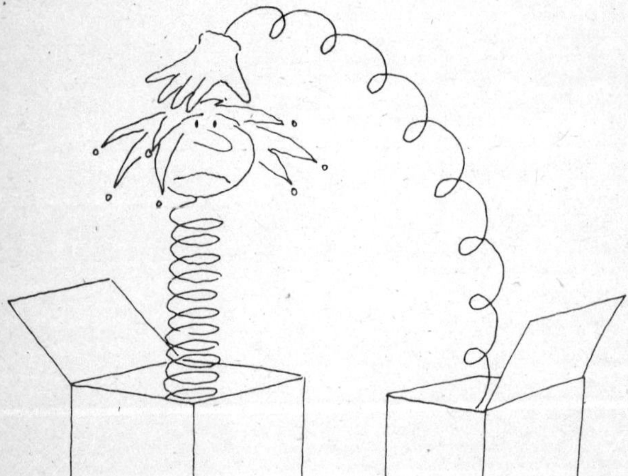
Nurit

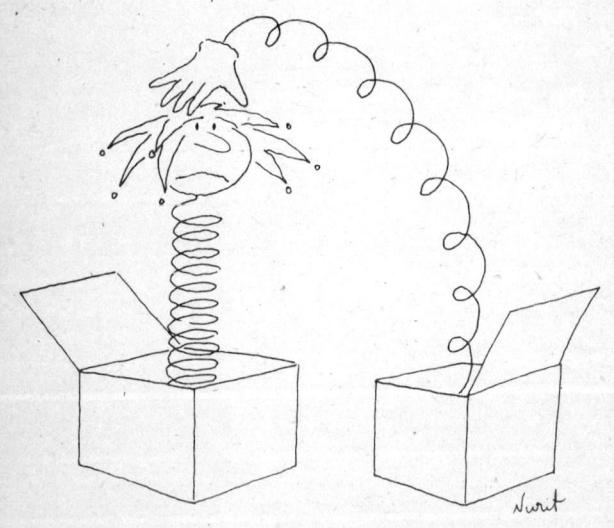

Nurit

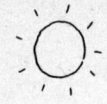

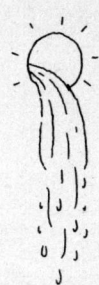

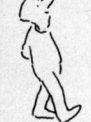

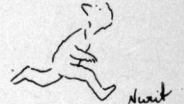

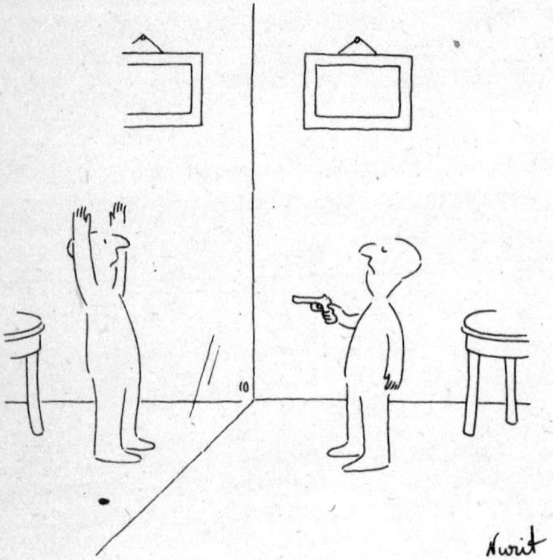
Nurit

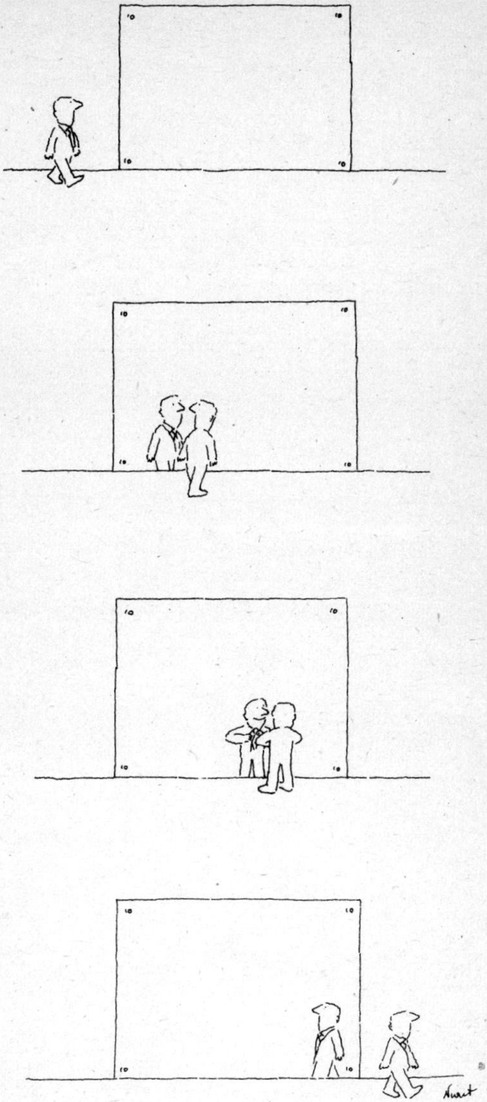

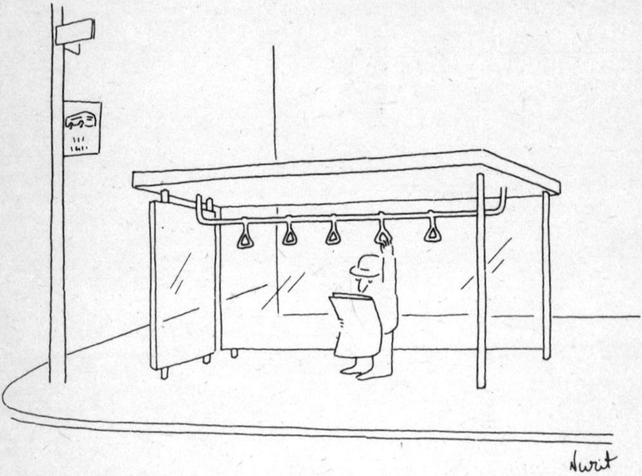
Nurit

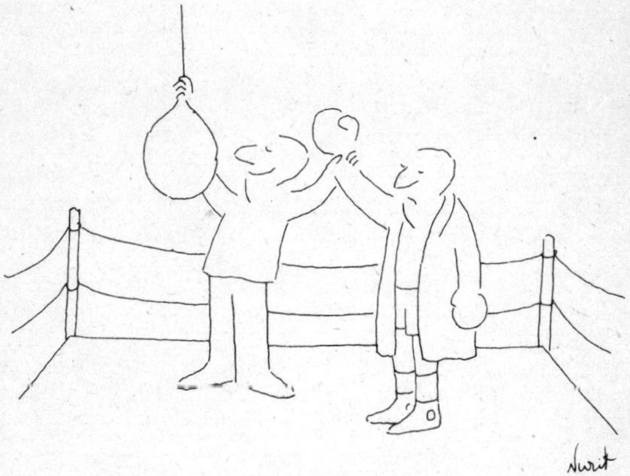
Nurit

PLOP
Nurit

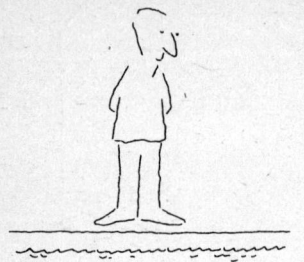

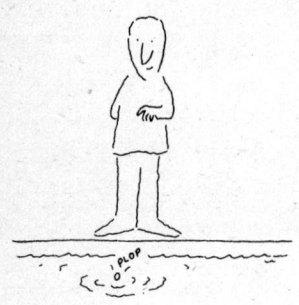

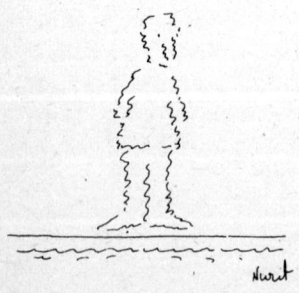

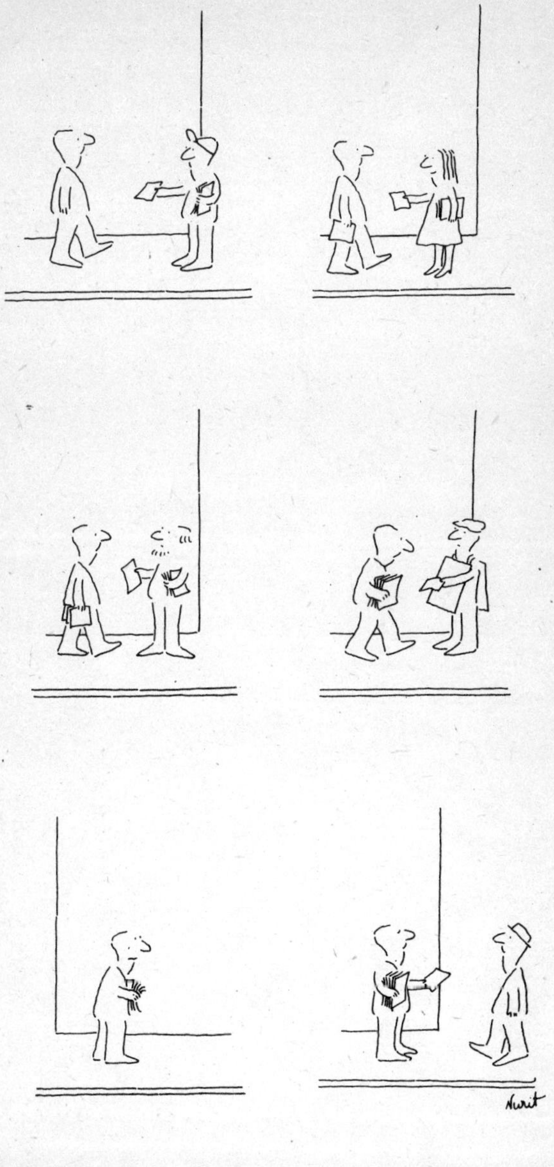
Nurit

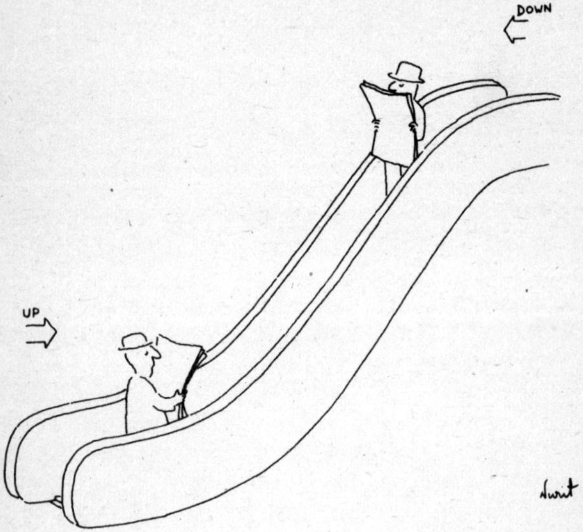
DOWN
UP
Nurit

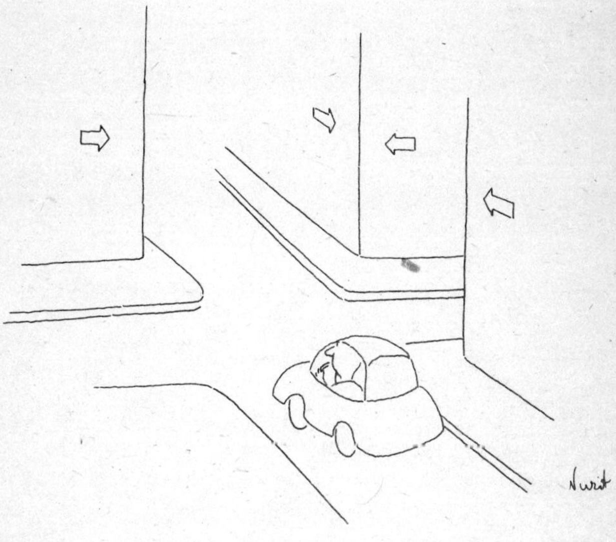
Nurit

Nurit

Nurit

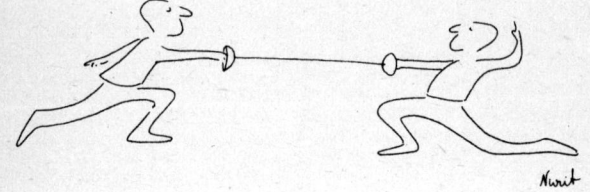

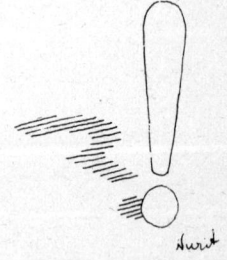

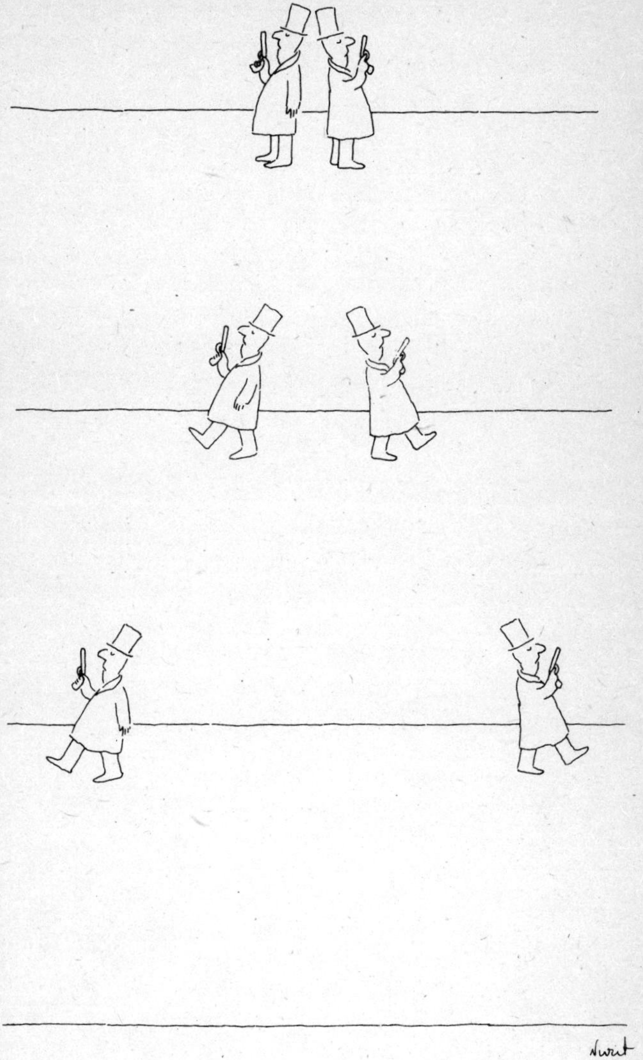
Nurit

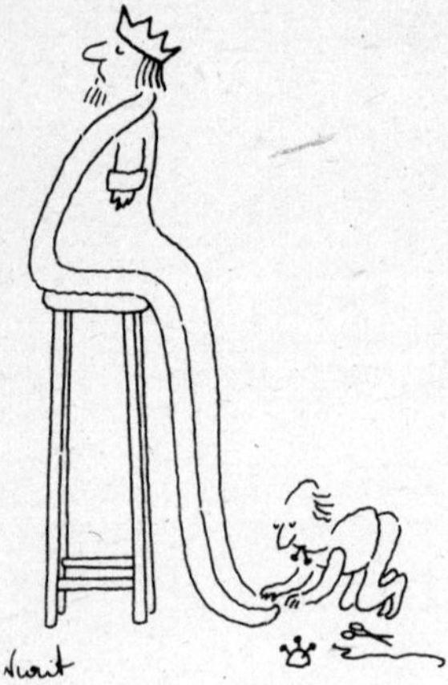
Nurit

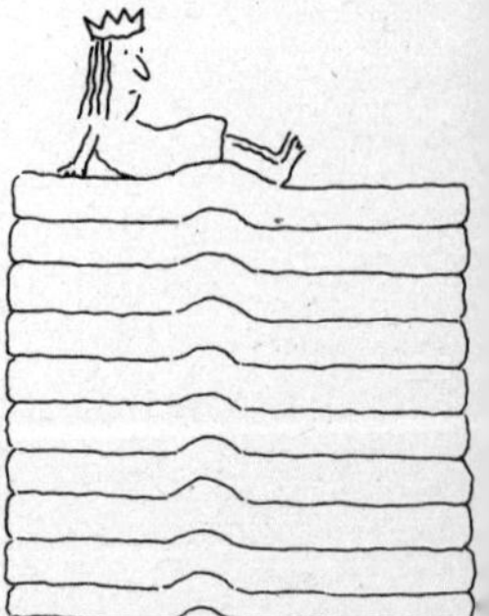

Nurit

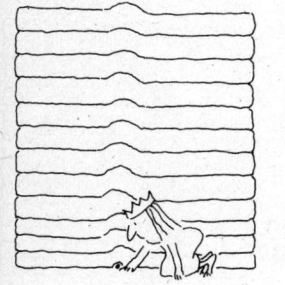

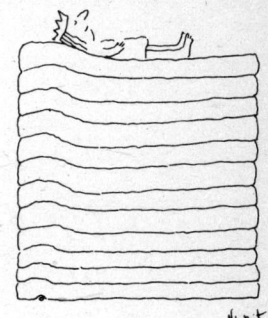

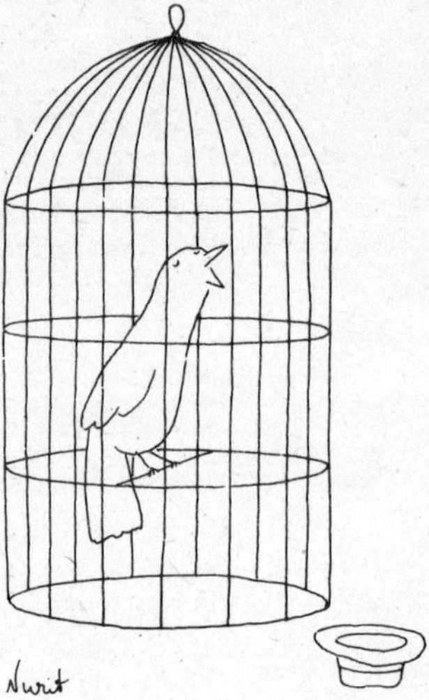
Nurit

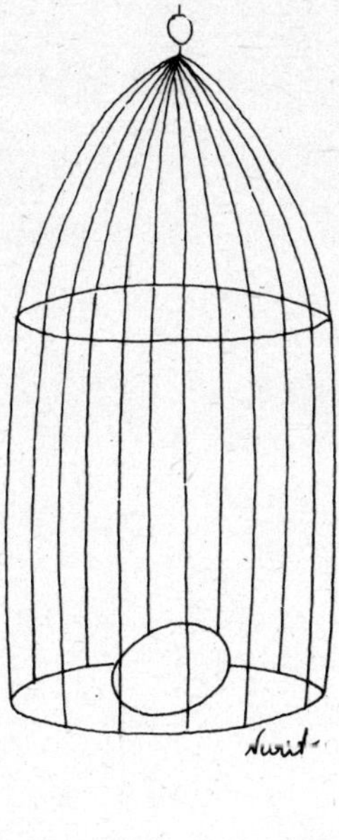
Nurit

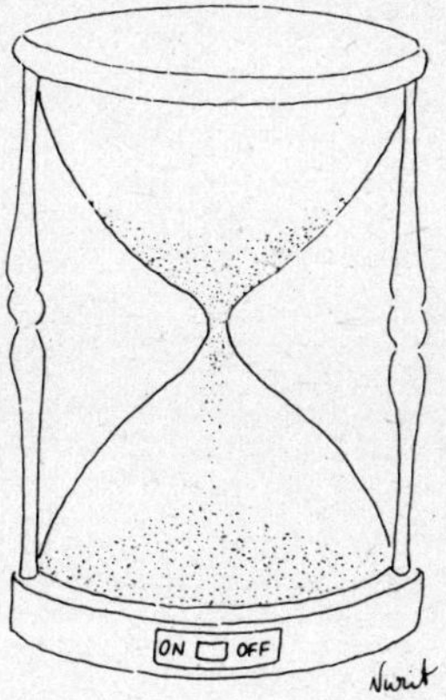
ON OFF
Nurit

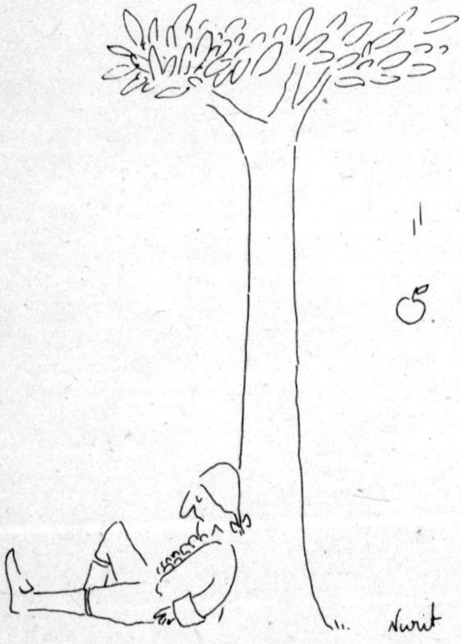
Nurit

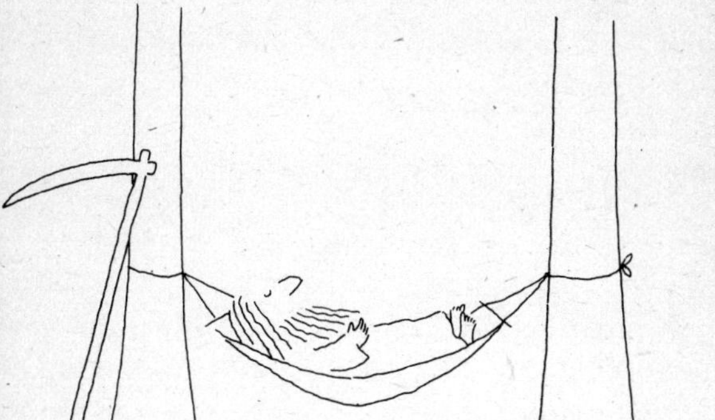
Nurit

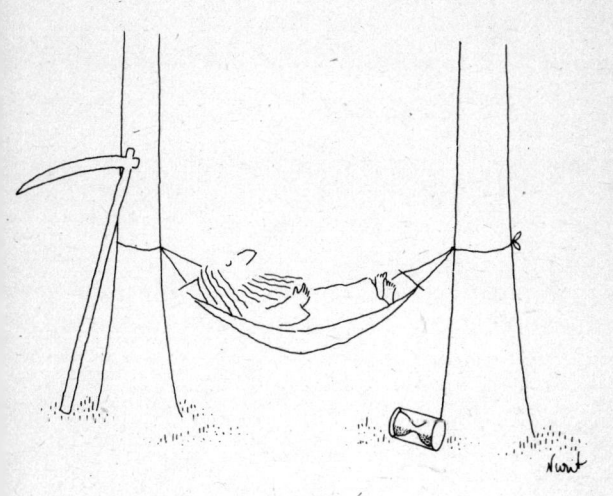

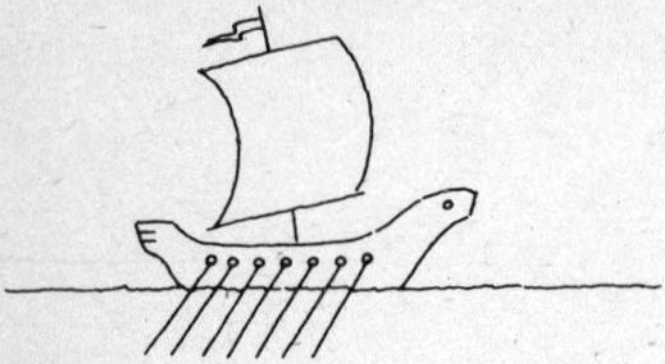

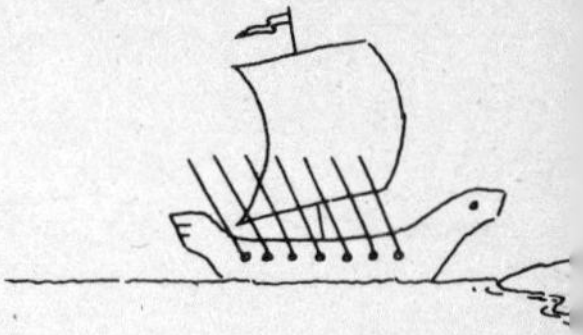

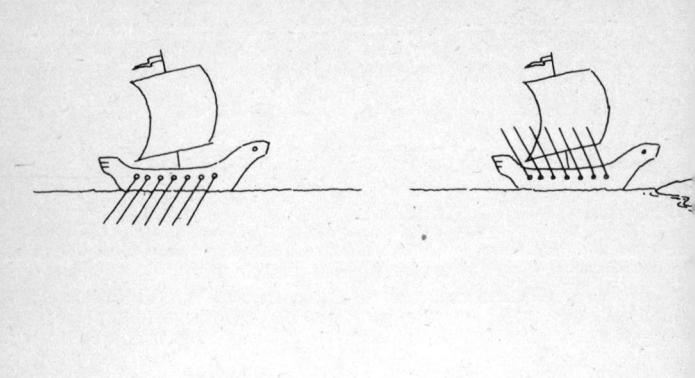

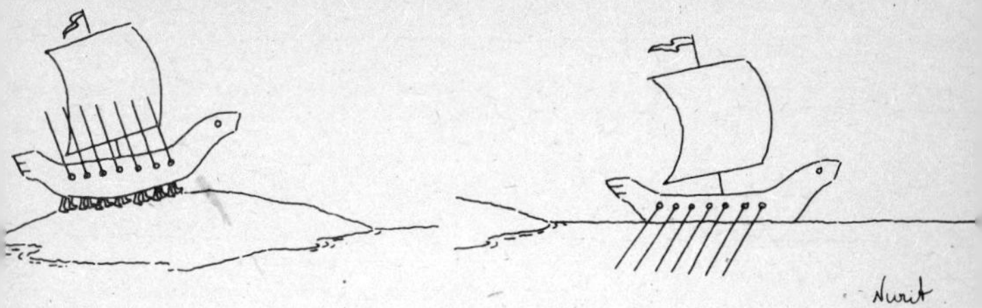
Nurit

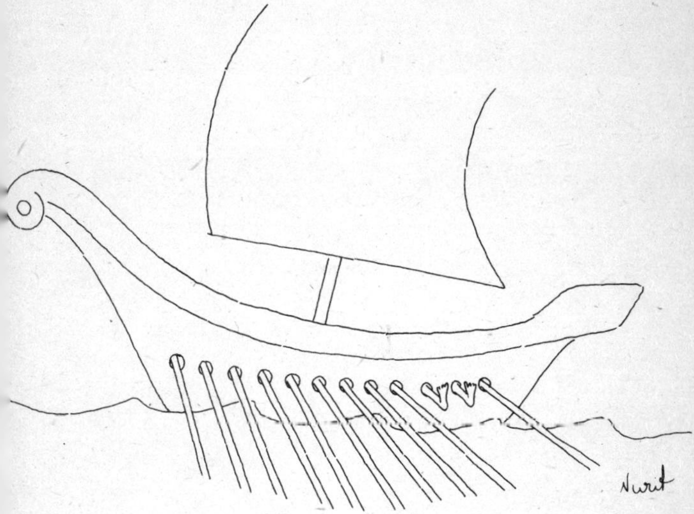
Nurit

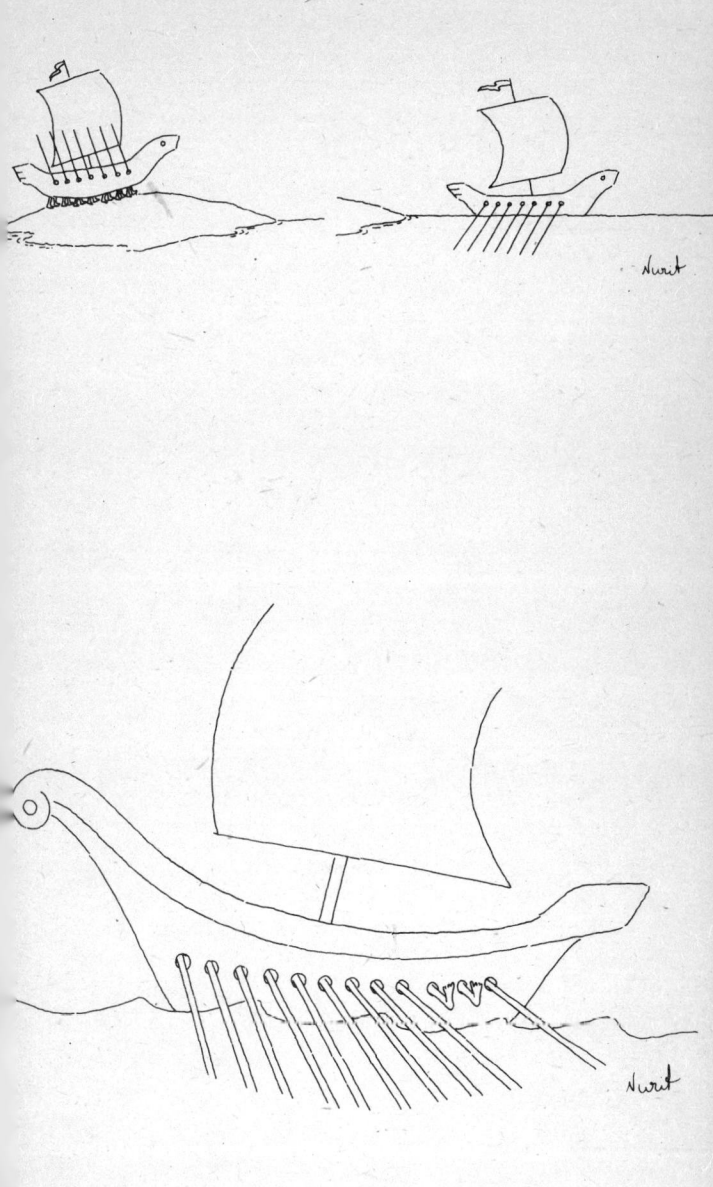

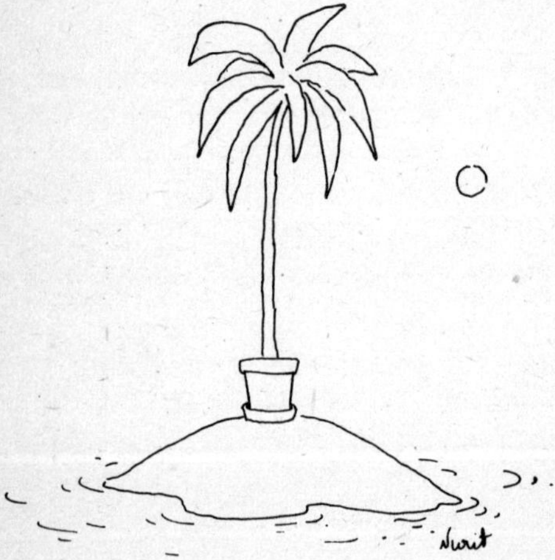
Nurit

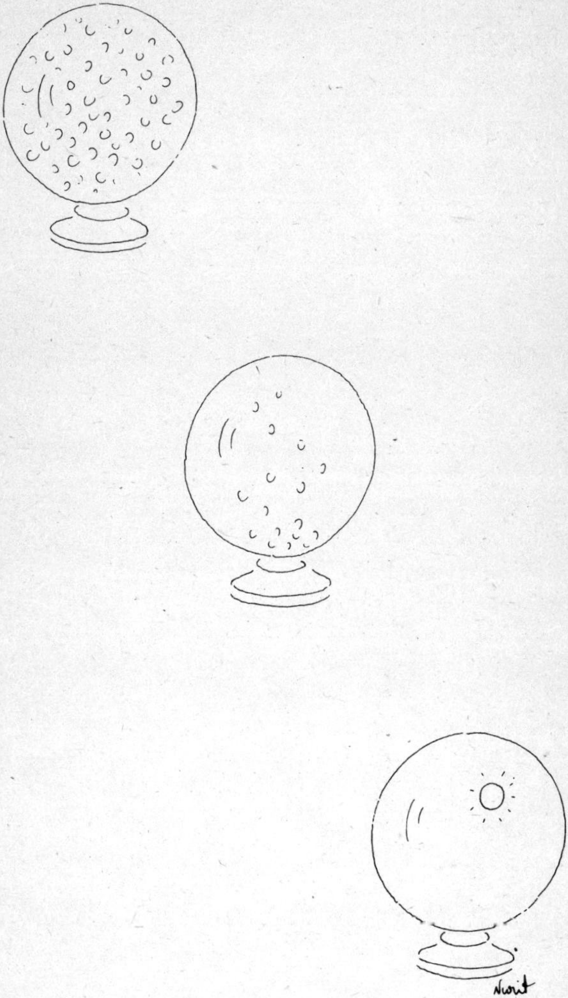
Nurit

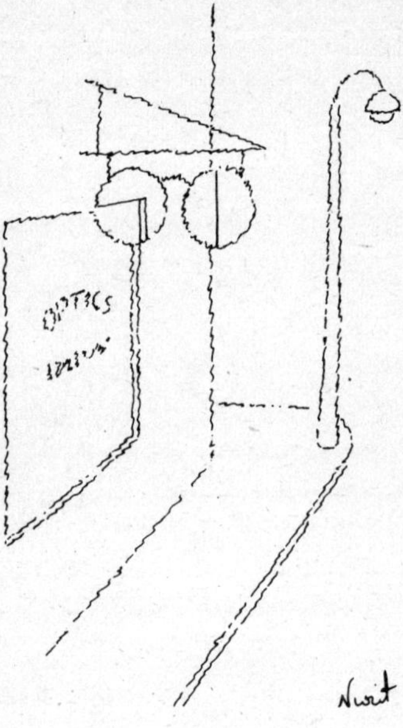
OPTICS
Nurit

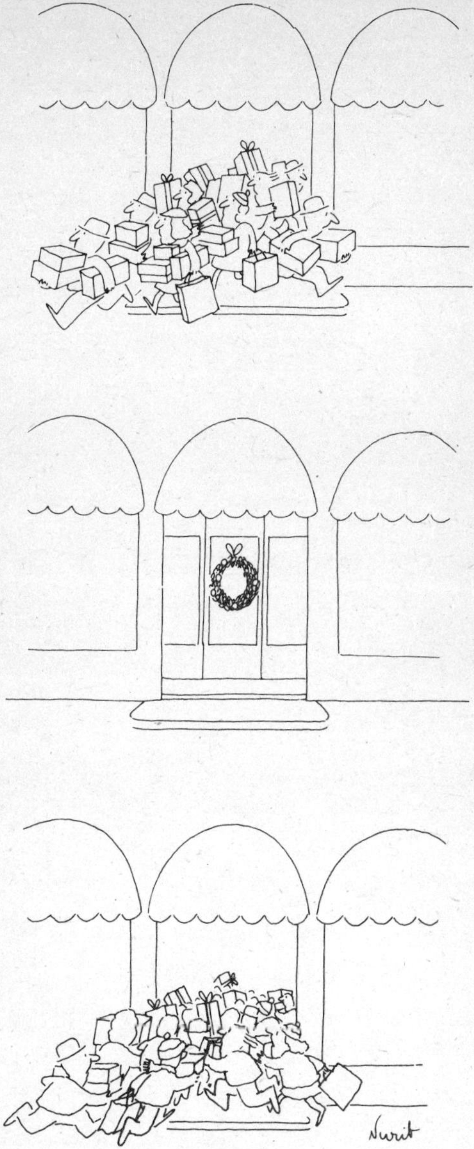
Nurit

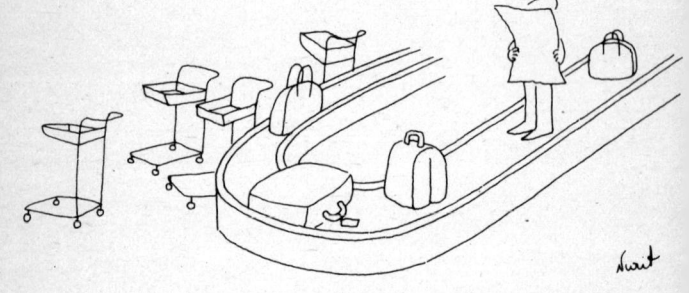

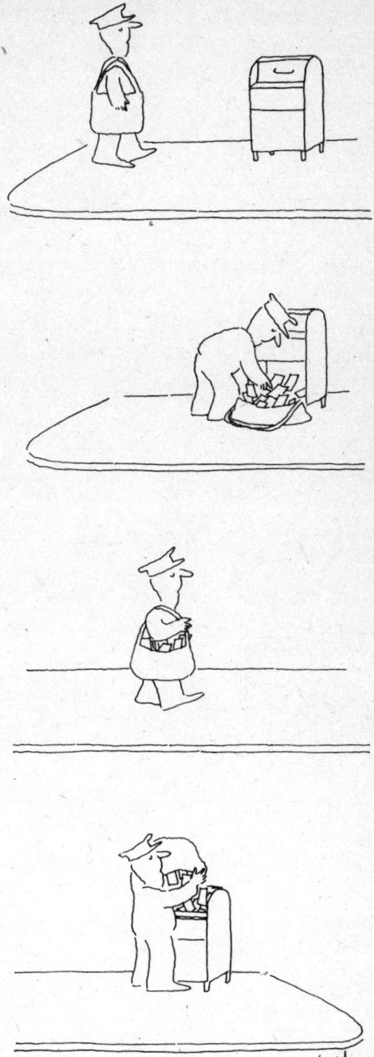
Nurit

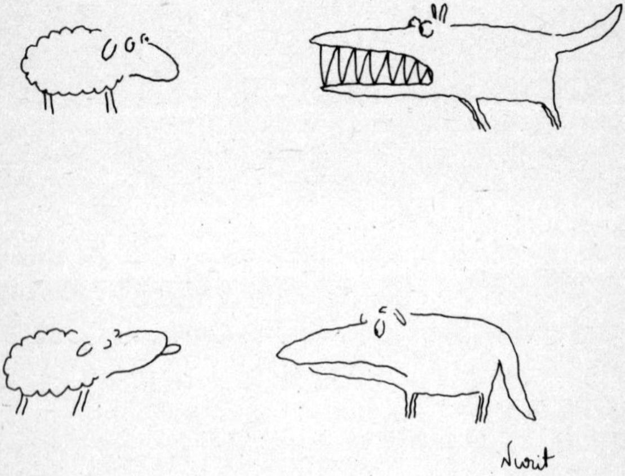
Nurit

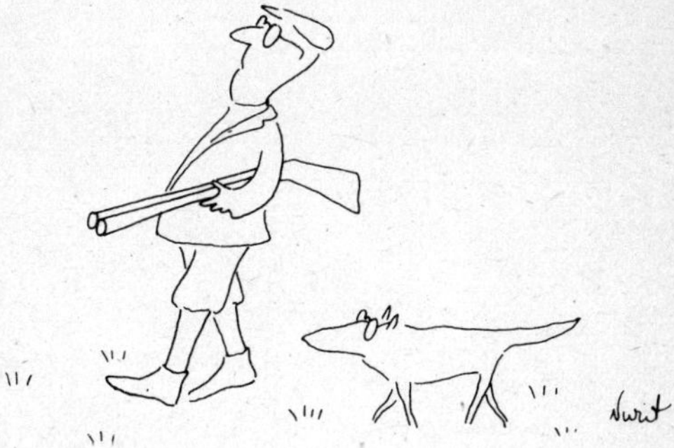
Nurit

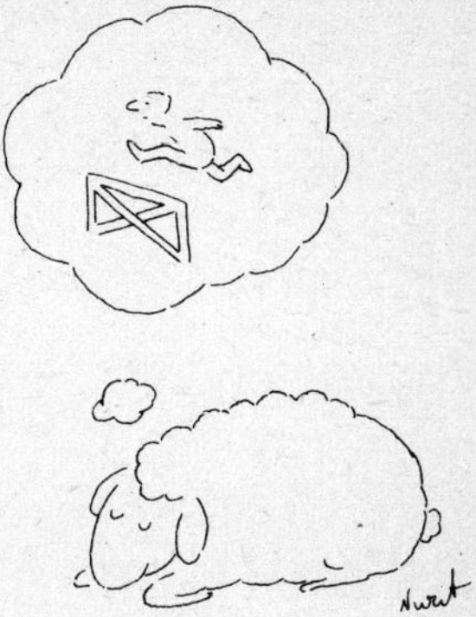
Nurit

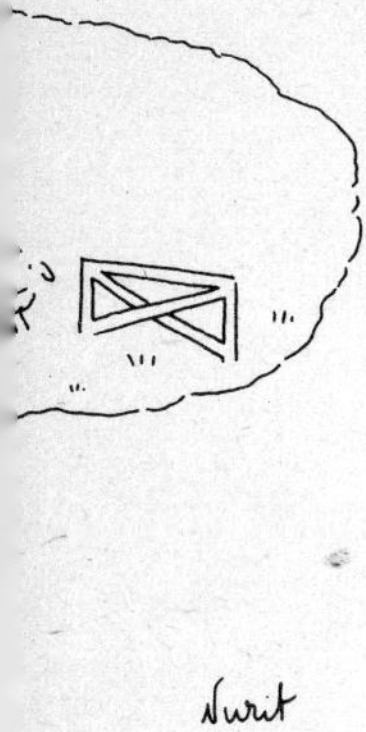
Nurit

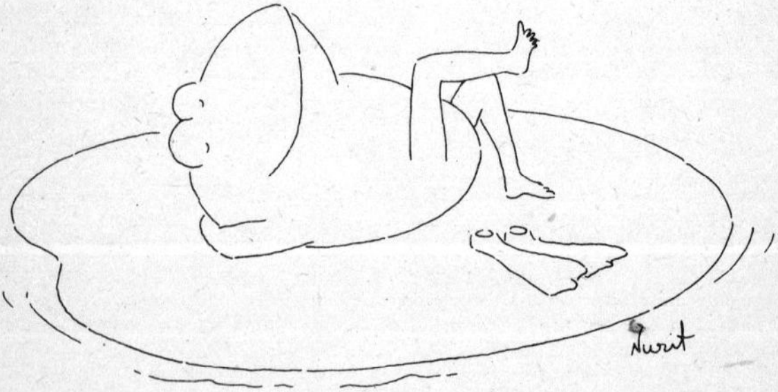
Nurit

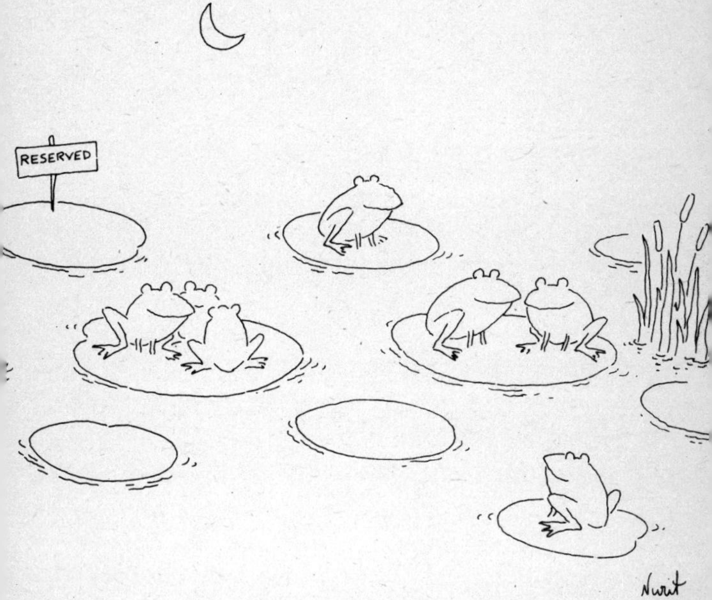
RESERVED
Nurit

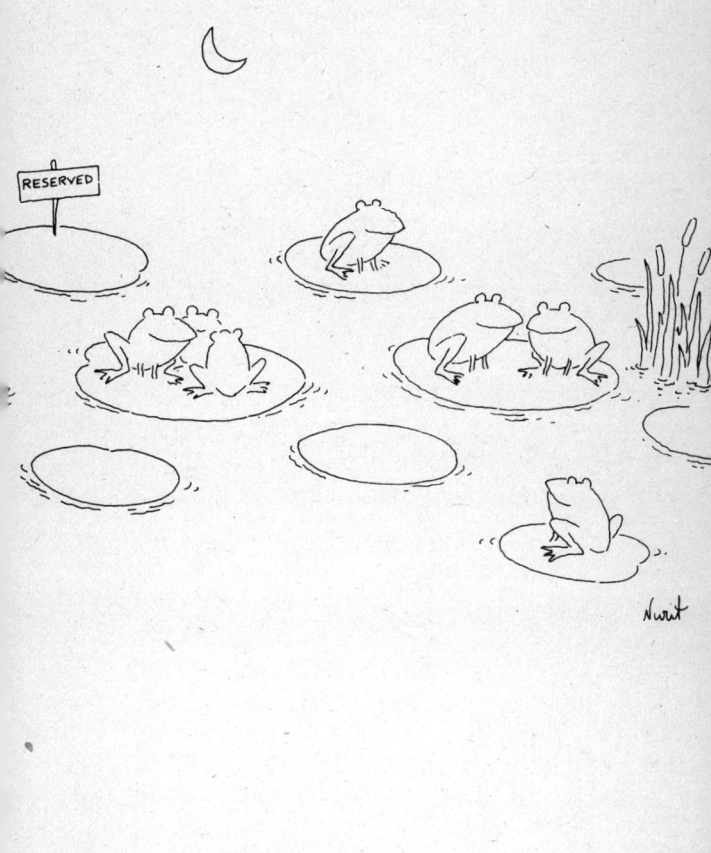

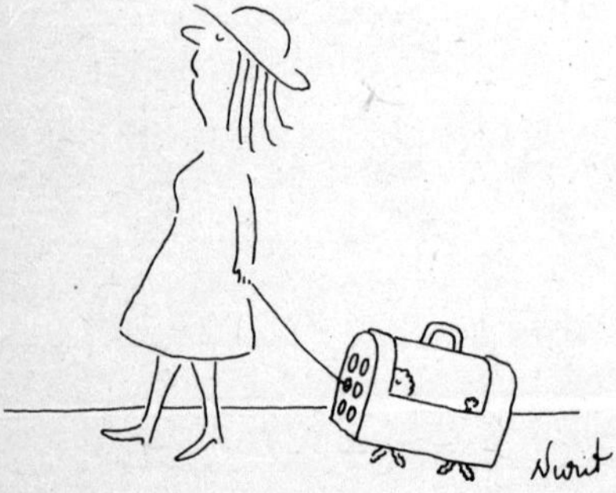
Nurit

Nurit

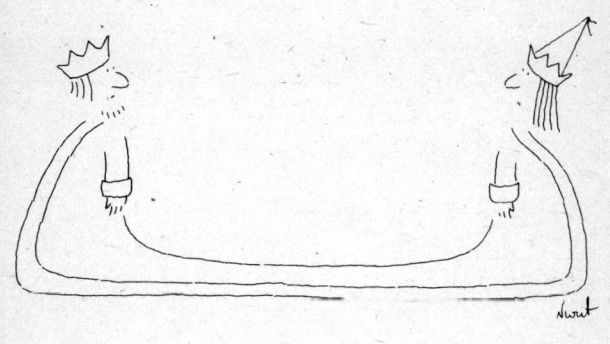

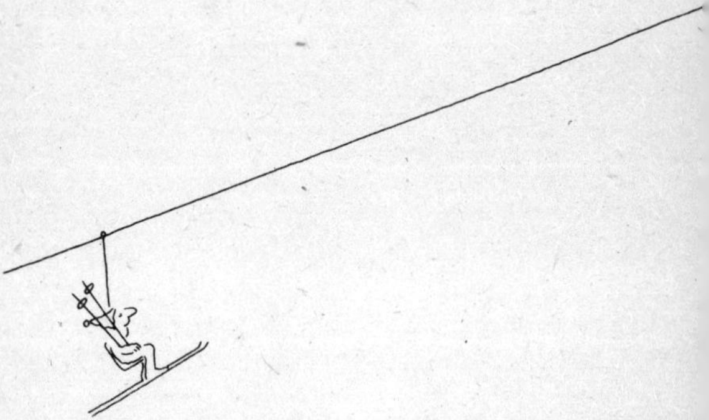

DAWSON SKI HILL